Dog Mama

Dog Mama

200 Tips, Trends, and How-To Secrets for Stylish Dog Owners

Serena Faber-Nelson

Skyhorse Publishing

Skyhorse Publishing books may be purchased in bulk at special discounts for sales promotion, corporate gifts, fund-raising, or educational purposes. Special editions can also be created to specifications. For details, contact the Special Sales Department, Skyhorse Publishing, 307 West 36th Street, 11th Floor, New York, NY 10018 or info@skyhorsepublishing.com.

Skyhorse® and Skyhorse Publishing® are registered trademarks of Skyhorse Publishing, Inc.®, a Delaware corporation.

Visit our website at www.skyhorsepublishing.com.

10 9 8 7 6 5 4 3 2 1

Library of Congress Cataloging-in-Publication Data is available on file.

Cover design by Daniel Brount
Cover photo by Alexander Mayes Photography (alexandermayesphotography.com)

Print ISBN: 978-1-5107-4472-1
Ebook ISBN: 978-1-5107-4474-5

Printed in China

Disclaimer: The author and publisher will not be held liable for the use or misuse of the information in this book. Before making any changes or additions to your dog's diet or lifestyle, remember to check with your local vet regarding your dog's individual needs.

For Emmy and Isobel

Contents

Introduction   xi

The 6 Types of Dog Moms   1
Living with Dogs   15
Health & Well-Being   57
Dog Photography   97
Pet Travel   133
Milestones & Entertaining   165
The Dog Directory   199

Credits   209
Thank You   215
About the Author   217

Introduction

~~Diamonds~~ Dogs are a girl's best friend

There's a good reason that so many dogs on social media have millions more followers than our regular human accounts: we love dogs.

In the pet-parenting boom over the last decade we've seen the rise of the "dog mom."—women who unashamedly treat their dogs like kids and incorporate them into their daily lives. But we're not the cast from *Best in Show*.

We are stylish, smart, influential women—who simply cherish and value the bonds we have with our dogs.

From organic treats, to luxe bedding, and on-trend fashion, dog mamas want the best for our pups. For dog moms, our pets are essentially extensions of ourselves.

From first loves, to first jobs, marriages, milestones, and beyond, our dogs grow with us as our confidants and best friends.

Dog Mama is not a training or behavior book. I'm not Cesar Millan (my dog still sleeps on the sofa when he thinks I'm not looking). Nor is this a photo book filled with cute dog shots (though there are plenty of those!). This book is a road map for dog moms to live their best lives with their pups.

Over the last two decades my job has seen me learn more dog tips and tricks than I could have ever imagined. In 2010 I started *Pretty Fluffy*—an online home for the stylish, modern pet owner. Through interviewing experts, reviewing products, and creating pet-parent-focused content, I've been steadily filling every corner of my brain with dog-related knowledge.

This book is all about breaking down this information into bite-sized pieces and sharing it with you—in the hope it will make life with your dog sweeter and easier.

This book is for you, dog mama. Enjoy . . . and give your dog a cuddle from me.

−Serena Faber-Nelson

The 6 Types of Dog Moms

The Active Dog Mom

Want to find an active dog mom in her natural habitat? Head to the local dog park. If you go before 7:00 a.m., you may even find a full herd of active dog moms.

This dog mama and her pup have energy to spare (it's like they regularly exercise and are filled with endorphins or something!). Get chatting and you'll hear all about their weekend fun runs, their adventurous hikes, and their daily games of fetch (they take turns with their pupper because it keeps both their heart rates up.)

They know all the latest fitness crazes for doggos . . . they're regulars at doga (dog yoga), doggy bootcamp (where you both get abs of steel), and pup-friendly paddleboarding.

For active dog moms, active wear is actual clothes they wear to exercise in—not just stretchy pants they wear with claims "they might go for a run later" (like some people who will remain nameless . . . cough, cough . . .)

Bursting with endless enthusiasm and great ideas of outdoor activities for dogs, the active dog mama is a fabulous friend to have around—they might even inspire you to break out of your comfort zone!

Just keep the fact that you and your dog spent last weekend on the couch binging Netflix to yourself.

The Dog Momager

Step aside, Kris Jenner.

The dog momager is the fierce talent behind every cute pupper you see on the 'gram. She's not a regular dog mom, she's a fun dog mom—and she has the 7,984 posts to prove it. (#blessed)

Armed with her trusty smartphone, you'll catch her on a random street corner waiting for the good light to come back while she snaps pics of her much-loved pup in their latest outfit (#woofcouture #gifted, of course). If you're lucky you may even get a glimpse of the oft-talked-about but never seen "Instagram husband" who has taken the afternoon off work to help them capture the perfect shot.

A dog momager knows "Daisy the Cavoodle" (105K followers, thank you very much) works best after an organic treat and belly rub. She lives and breathes in hashtags and has memorized the best filters to edit out dog hair.

While her parents lament the chosen use of her PR degree, the dog momager is laughing all the way to the bank. Want to know the hottest new dog trends? Want to see the cutest collars? This girl's your gal.

We'd all love to hate on her, but the pull of her sublime photos and witty captions is just too strong. So we double tap that cuteness and wait with bated breath for the next post.

The Designer Dog Mom

Want to know who's got a better wardrobe than you? A designer dog mom's dog, that's who.

The designer dog mom knows her Burberry from her Balenciaga, and her Louis Vuitton from her Louboutins (the latter she keeps far away from her dog's reach!).

With a fashionable eye, this dog mama nearly always looks like she's stepped off the cover of *Vogue* . . . or should that be *Dogue*?

This stylish pair always make it work. For casual Thursdays they do matching gingham. For more formal occasions it's a bespoke monogrammed clutch for her and a bespoke monogrammed collar for pooch . . . and, of course, on Wednesdays, they wear pink.

The designer dog mom is never seen without a perfect blowout (for both dog and mom) and has a seemingly endless rotation of outfits that has you, and your pup, drooling for more. We're pretty sure her wardrobe's net value is worth more than our apartment.

You'll find this pair surfing Net-a-Porter, hiding their online order boxes from their significant others, and just generally looking more fabulous than everybody else. Don't hate them because they're beautiful.

The "I Like My Dog More than My Kids" Dog Mom

This mom has a favorite child and it's no secret.

While her kids harass her for whose turn it is to use the iPad, this dog mama knows her trusty pooch will let her have a bath in peace.

The early morning walk with her four-legged friend is this mom's favorite part of the day. That, and cuddling up on the sofa together watching *Outlander* in the evening. (Dad worked out long ago that the dog gets first dibs on the comfiest part of the lounge.)

This dog mama loves to spoil her pooch with new toys and treats, and has no shame in pampering her "third child" who doesn't talk back. She'll spend hours making her pup a superfood, dietician approved dinner . . . and then order a pizza for everyone else.

See a message notification from this dog mama, and you know it's a meme about parenting. Check her "Stay at Home Dog Mom" coffee mug, and you may just find it's filled with wine.

But you know what? This mom is the first person you'll turn to when you need advice on kids or dogs—she knows it all. And, quietly, she loves her kids (furry and non-furry) more than anything in the world.

The Rescue Dog Mom

With "Adopt Don't Shop" emblazoned across her tee, you know exactly what you're getting with the rescue dog mom.

These dog mamas are all about saving and helping dogs in need. It doesn't matter that they live in a studio apartment and their landlord has given them two written warnings about no more pets.

The rescue dog mom started early. She was the girl who brought home the dog she found on the walk home from school and begged her parents to keep it. (Everyone later discovered it was Betty Schneider's cocker spaniel from down the street. Betty had been frantic with worry for the last twenty-four hours–whoopsie!)

Does a rescue dog mom judge you for not getting your dog from the shelter? Probably a little bit, but she'll never say. She'll just tag you in photo after photo of cute shelter pups looking for a home until you give in.

By joining the rescue dog mom ranks, you'll soon learn the secret they all know: Opening up your home to a shelter dog gives that pooch a whole new life *and* you get a best friend in return!

Rescue dog moms are filled with patience, kindness, and a whole lot of love, and the world would be a pretty awesome place if there were more of them around.

The Organic Dog Mom

Get chatting with an organic dog mom, and in ten minutes you'll know more about the benefits of coconut oil than you ever thought possible.

Armed with a green smoothie and her reusable shopping bag, you'll find her at her local farmers' market stocking up on essentials for the week with her trusty pooch by her side. She'll walk you through which fruit and veggies are clean and which are the Dirty Dozen in seconds flat.

Owing to a homemade diet packed with superfoods, her hair is silky and shiny, her eyes are bright, and her smile is perfection . . . and that's just her dog we're talking about.

Processed food doesn't pass the lips of her or her pooch—or if it does, you'll need photographic evidence before she'll admit it. She'll swear by the healing properties of apple cider vinegar, and you'll be blown away when some of her tips actually work a treat!

Don't be fooled by her glowing, peaceful demeanor. This is one switched-on mama who can inspire you and your dog to be more health-conscious and environmentally friendly.

Just get used to hearing a lot about essential oils.

Living with Dogs

Setting Up the Perfect Pet-Friendly Home

I got my first dog when I graduated college. Now, while some Insta-famous twenty-year-olds have stylish homes, money to burn, and a knack for interior decorating, I sadly did not. My dog pretty much slept on my bed, had a collar from the local pet store (I think it was plain black?), and both of us considered IKEA the epitome of home style (oh hello, wavy mirrors!). Our first home certainly wasn't pet-friendly and it certainly wasn't stylish. But the great thing about knowing nothing? The only way is up.

At the time, I got my first job working on a travel television program. Dream job, right? Not for me. I wanted to move across the hall to work on the pet show. And a year later I did, where my voracious appetite for all things pet-related started. I read, interviewed experts, learned everything I could, and bit by bit my knowledge base started to grow.

Fast-forward to now, and I can name luxury dog beds off the top of my head, tell you the best way to protect your sofa from paw prints, and give you the pros and cons of that dog bowl you're thinking of buying. In short, I can set up a pet-friendly home in no time. And with these tips it's totally easy for you to do so, too.

Whether you've just gotten your first dog, or you have a faithful companion of many years, there's no time better than now to make your home pet-friendly.

What do I mean by pet-friendly? I certainly don't mean having dog products invade every corner of your space, or making your home decor paw print-themed.

A true pet-friendly home is all about including your dog in your home environment without sacrificing your own personal style. With minimal effort, you can easily have a magazine-worthy home with your dog.

1. Know Your Dog

When starting out, the first place to focus is your dog themselves. Ask yourself these questions to really get to know the spaces your dog uses, the products they need, and the mess they bring!

- Are they mainly an inside or outside dog?
- What rooms do they have access to?
- Do they bring pet hair, paw prints, or other mess inside?
- Where do they eat, play, and sleep?
- Are they more of a *Real Housewives* fan or do they prefer true crime documentaries? (Joking, we all know dogs love a bit of *Housewives*.)

Once you've answered these, you'll pinpoint the areas to focus on and any issues to address.

2. Choose a Color Scheme

Any interior designer worth their salt will tell you: every home starts with a color scheme. And that includes your pet products!

I've lost count of the number of times I've entered a beautifully styled home, only to see a shabby brown bed thrown hastily in a corner and a bright red plastic dog bowl sitting next to the kitchen counter. By all means, I'd never judge a person on their choice of dog bowl, but if you're making an effort with the rest of your home, don't stop at the pet supplies.

Years ago we barely had any options, but these days a treasure trove of low- and high-end pet products are made well and are aesthetically pleasing, and they fit any and every interior theme.

To get started with a color scheme, take a look at the main pieces in any given room. If your vibe is monochromatic, choose black and white pet accessories that match. A fan of grays? Look for blush-accented dog bowls to add the perfect accent color.

By general rule, a room's color palette should have one main color (i.e., walls), one secondary color (large furnishings, rugs, etc,), and a few accent colors and textures that bring them all together. One expert tip is to start with a piece you love—be it an artwork, rug, or wallpaper—and draw your color palette from there.

Whatever pieces you choose, extending your color scheme to your pet supplies allows them to integrate seamlessly into your home.

3. Opt for Pet-Friendly Furnishings

When choosing major pieces for your home, always consider how pet-friendly they are. If your dog is allowed to snooze on the sofa, opt for neutral fabrics that are durable and/or washable. And get the Scotchgard. Always. These days there are so many options of microfiber fabrics, performance velvets, and stain resistant covers that you can expect form and function from your lounge (ain't nobody got time for scrubbing the sofa every weekend).

The same goes for floor rugs. Choose rugs that can survive stains and regular vacuuming. With an increasing number of dog-loving designers these days, many furniture outlets have specific pet-friendly collections. Take advantage and get a look you love (that your dog won't ruin).

4. Don't Be Afraid of White

While muddy paw prints on a white sofa might be the stuff of nightmares, white can be all right . . . in fact, sometimes white is easier to clean than other colors. When you're looking at sheets, bedding, and removable slipcovers, white soft furnishings are actually quite easy to keep fresh and pristine.

Many people use bleach to keep their whites whiter than white, but a gentler option is to use natural cleaners to get out any doggie stains. Add half a cup of baking soda with your detergent at the beginning of the wash cycle, then, at the start of the rinse cycle, pour in half a cup of white vinegar.

Pro Tip!

A good quality floor cushion can pull double duty as a dog bed. With the large number of cushions on the market in a range of budgets, you'll always have an option to match your home aesthetic. Just ensure the filling is comfortable and supportive for sleep.

5. The Bed Is Everything

I often get asked where pet owners should scrimp and where they should spend on pet supplies. And my answer every time? Spend on the bed.

Just like us, dogs need a good bed to sleep in, relax, and somewhere to call their very own. (And you know if you don't give them their own bed, they'll be taking yours.) Because even the smallest dog beds aren't small—they unwittingly become a major feature of a room whether you like it or not.

Invest in a dog bed that has classic lines, durable materials, and a sophisticated palette (step away from the paw prints!). Look for hypoallergenic foam fillings and washable exteriors that make for comfy dozing and easy cleaning.

A quality dog bed will stand the test of time and will be an investment you won't regret.

6. Opt for Quality Materials

The materials you choose for your pet supplies will literally make or break your quest for a stylish, pet-friendly home. Poorly made beds, collars, and bowls will just cost you time and money in the long run as they will easily tear, wear, and disintegrate with use.

What you want to look for is durable, practical, yet stylish finishes. Heavy-duty cotton, leather, and brass finishings all offer a luxe feel while putting up with everything your dog throws at them (be that slobber, dirt, and multiple attempts to rip apart!).

For the bed, look for dark hues or patterns if your dog tends to bring muddy paw prints everywhere he goes. Collars and leashes need strong, safe clasps and tough, quality fabrics that not only look good but keep your pup safe.

7. Dine in Style

Dog food and water bowls are often the forgotten piece of the puzzle.

Firstly, you need to be practical—think, does your dog eat and drink inside or outside? Do they need multiple sets of bowls? Do they have a tendency to knock over their water bowl? Do they need a raised feeder?

Ceramic bowls are beautiful yet totally functional go-to options. Weighted on the bottom, they're too heavy to knock over or move around. Plus, the glazed finish gives a luxe, timeless quality other bowls just don't have.

There are so many stunning bowl designs these days that they can easily work within any modern home. (So stylish you'll consider eating out of them!)

8. Have a Dedicated Pet Station

"A place for everything and everything in it's place." Your grandma didn't tell you that for no reason. One of the easiest ways to keep your home looking beautiful is to have a dedicated storage area for your pet's things.

Grooming products, lint rollers, and apparel can all be stored neatly in a dedicated shelf or basket. Choose a spot tucked away out of sight, but easily accessible. That way you no longer have random pet products cluttering up your living space.

Woven baskets make great hidden-in-plain-sight toy storage, whereas beautifully crafted collars and leashes can hang proudly on display. Got a stunning, handmade leash? Hang that baby in plain sight and let people see how lovely it is!

9. Make Throws Your Friend

Any seasoned dog mama will know: throws make a stylish pet-friendly home possible.

Pop them on your lounge, on the foot of your bed, anywhere that needs a bit of extra protection. A well-placed throw (matching the color scheme you've chosen, of course) hides a multitude of sins, protects your furniture, *and* adds a stylish textural element to any room.

Faux hides and fur throws evoke a timeless, luxe feel and are also super comfortable for your pup, whereas chunky knits add texture and pops of color—all while working double duty to protect your furnishings from claws and paws.

THE ULTIMATE "DOG MAMA" PET-FRIENDLY HOME

1. A stylish doggy door to let them in and out.
2. A hidden doggy nook just for them.
3. A perfectly organized pet-friendly cupboard.
4. Hardwood floors to make picking up pet hair a breeze.
5. Furniture in neutral hues to disguise any little paw prints.
6. Dutch doors keep your dog in sight but out of no-go zones.
7. A family mudroom for cleaning muddy paws after a long walk.
8. A dedicated pet wash station.
9. A colorful outdoor area perfect for dog-friendly BBQs and gatherings.
10. A dog-friendly yard filled with green lawns for fetch, and shrubbery for sniffing.

    A girl can dream, right?

Handy Hint

For families with young puppies: this is a great project to revisit throughout the year, turning it into a keepsake work of art with their age written under each paw print.

DIY: Paw Print Wall Art

This easy project allows you to create your very own stylish artwork on a shoestring budget. In just a few minutes you'll have a personalized piece you can display for years to come.

You'll Need:

- 1 sheet of paper—choose a heavy paper stock
- Paintbrush
- Nontoxic washable paint in your chosen color
- Fine-tip ink pen
- Frame, sized to match your paper
- Your dog!

Prepping Tips:

Paint and dogs—What could go wrong? To prevent a puppy-Picasso-painted home, spread out an old sheet or tarp to protect your floors and furniture, or head outside.

Have a bowl filled with a hint of pet shampoo and warm water ready to wash off those little paws, and a towel to dry them.

Method:

1. With your chosen paint color, take the paintbrush and carefully paint your dog's paw pad. If your dog has ticklish paws, you may need an extra set of hands!
2. Gently press your dog's paw onto the paper. Press and hold for a couple of seconds and try to lift the paw straight up to ensure zero smudging. Let the paw print rest for about 10 minutes or until completely dry.
3. While your print is drying, wash your dog's paw with soapy water. Towel dry any excess water.
4. Once the paw print is dry, you can use a fine-tip ink pen to write their name and age underneath.
5. Frame and display.

Pet-Proofing Like a Pro

Before you become a dog mama, there are certain things that are a lot easier. After a late-night movie binge, there's no problem with chocolate remnants all over the sofa, socks thrown with abandon over the floor, and a half-eaten pizza on the coffee table.

But you're a dog mom now and with this great power also comes great responsibility. Not really. But there are a few things you can totally do to keep your pup *and* your stuff safe.

1. Keep food items out of reach.

This one sounds like a no-brainer, but when you live without dogs, it's just something you don't have to worry about. But once you have a dog? *Well.* Due to their amazing sense of smell—and an uncanny ability to sense food from two towns over—even the best-trained dogs will be extremely opportunistic. Not only does this ruin their balanced diet, but also a lot of human foods can be extremely harmful to dogs.

So it's best to ensure all food items are stored out of reach, including preparation utensils, plates, pet foods, mints and gums, and decorative food items. And by out of reach, I mean out of reach. Never underestimate a doggo's ability to get to food. They are wily little creatures. Same goes for after dinner, or random snacks on the sofa (see previously mentioned movie binges). You want to keep things out of your dog's reach and always tidy up after you've finished eating (or they will).

2. Safely store poisonous items and household chemicals.

Start in your kitchen and laundry, moving on to your bathroom, bedrooms, and garage, ensuring all cleaning products, medications, pesticides, car kits, batteries, and beauty products are put away out of reach. Even the most seemingly harmless items, such as herbal supplements, toothpaste, and hairspray cans, can be toxic and dangerous to dogs.

3. Cover your rubbish bins, laundry hampers, washing machines, and dishwashers.

All of these items carry significant scents that attract a dog's attention. By ensuring they are closed and/or covered your pooch can't break into them, causing mess or compromising their safety.

Once you're done, walk through your home and approach it from a dog's viewpoint. Are there things they'll want to chew, climb on, or investigate that may be dangerous? A quick look around will pick up anything you may have missed (you don't have to get down on all fours, but it wouldn't hurt!).

4. Keep electrical cords out of reach or safely secured.

For years this used to be as easy as securing the television, toaster, and iron cords and walking away. However with today's technology, you need to ensure laptop cords, phone chargers, and ethernet cords are also kept safely. If the cords are fixed, ensure they are secured where they cannot be reached. If the cords are used transiently throughout the house, get into the habit of packing them away whenever they are not in use.

5. Check your boundaries—inside and out.

If you have a backyard, scour the perimeter of fencing, checking for gaps and places where your dog could dig and get out. Also check the sturdiness and security of your gate. Close off staircases, balconies, and any open high spaces to prevent falls and injury. If you're not sure how to keep your pup contained, consider investing in a baby gate to limit their access to dangerous areas.

6. Declutter.

Let's #konmari up this place! Dogs explore with their mouths, so for their safety *and your sanity* place small items, breakables, and knickknacks out of reach. This includes your shoes (spoken from a devastated shoe lover who had more than five pairs destroyed before learning her lesson); choking-hazard items such as coins and pins, and sentimental pieces that can't be replaced.

Dogs don't generally care if something was your family heirloom—in fact I swear they find sentimental heirlooms and expensive shoes the tastiest of all (RIP family Christmas ornament passed down for three generations).

And don't underestimate the power of your pup's tail. Mugs, wineglasses, and expensive coffee-table decor are no match for tail power. If your dog's tail can reach it, best be moving it.

7. Make your garden pet-friendly.

Pooches love the outdoors, and if you're lucky enough to have a garden, your dog has years of frolicking to enjoy. Go through your garden ensuring any plants that may be poisonous to your new pup are removed or securely protected. Same goes for your beloved indoor plants.

PET-FRIENDLY PLANTS

Of *course* it's the way that some of the most beautiful and popular plants you see frequenting the Instagram feeds of the stylish and amazing are toxic to dogs. This is why I have no indoor plants. (Definitely not because I seem to be unable to keep anything green alive. That's not the reason *at all*.) For a full list of plants toxic to pets, ask your local vet or ASPCA Poison Control.

Popular Indoor Plants Toxic for Dogs
Fiddle-leaf fig
Crassula ovata (also known as jade plant)
Zamioculcas (also known as ZZ plant)
Aloe vera
Monstera

Popular Outdoor Plants Toxic for Dogs
Hydrangeas
Tulips
Daffodils
Oleander
Peonies

Is that dog hair in the fridge? How to Stay Pet-Hair Free

Hanging in my wardrobe is a tee that says "Dog Hair, Don't Care." But do you know what? As a self-confessed neat freak, I do actually care. I care a lot.

In fact, dog hair is up there in being one of the peeviest of pet peeves of pet owners. Even owners of so-called non-shedding breeds are not entirely immune. Dog fur and dander gets on your clothes, on your furniture, in your car, and generally will blow around like tumbleweeds across your living room if you don't get control of it.

The reality is, dogs come with lots of hair and most of that ends up throughout your home. So that pretty much leaves you with two choices:

A) Start a business making weird sculptures out of pet hair.
B) Follow my three-step program to get pet-hair free. (I'll even throw in a free set of steak knives!*)

---

* No I won't.

It All Starts with a Clean Dog

The number one thing you can do to prevent pet hair building up in your home is to regularly groom your dog. That means regular brushing and monthly grooming (see my tips for Grooming Like a Boss on page 77).

If you've ever seen how much hair can come out of just one full body brush, you'll understand why your home is currently covered in fur. The same goes for regular bathing—whether you wash your dog at home or take her to a professional.

For an interesting experiment—next time your dog gets a full wash and groom, give your home a deep clean. In the days that follow you'll notice minimal dog hair and dander on your floors, clothes, and furniture—simply because so much of the dead hair has been washed away! Now don't waste this glorious time. Continue to brush daily.

Invest in the Best Tools You Can

Now, while you've reduced the amount of dog hair your pup is shedding, I'd be kidding you if I said that was all you needed to do. The second step involves cleaning the dog hair that your pooch does shed—with the absolute minimum amount of time and effort. Because I don't know about you, but I'd prefer to be lying on my couch watching *Nailed It* rather than picking dog hair off it.

The number one tool in your dog hair arsenal is the best pet hair vacuum you can afford. Sure, there are a whole host of "quick

Pro Tip!

A good blow dry at the groomers can get rid of a lot of excess dead hair—especially for dogs with undercoats.

fix" brooms, "amazing" fabric sweepers, and "As Seen on TV" pet hair mitts—but they all involve an investment of time and often only clean one element, such as hardwood floors, or fabric sofas.

A quality vacuum and a well-set-up home (see my tips in Setting Up the Perfect Pet-Friendly Home on page 17) is all you need. Depending on the size of your apartment or house I would suggest a choosing one or a combination of the below four types of vacuums to keep pet hair under control:

Cordless Stick Vacuum: Cordless vacuums have come such a long way in the last few years that for small spaces, they can be the only vacuum cleaner you need. Current cordless pet hair vacuums are designed to eliminate pet hair and allergens throughout your home—and they don't have the hassle of dragging round a heavy turbine and tangled cord! Current stick vacuums are lightweight and have long battery lives, meaning you can often clean your whole living space in one go. These babies are great for quick daily cleans and keeping pet hair under control as you go with minimal fuss.

2-in-1 Vac & Steam Cleaners: Just like the cordless vacuum, these cleaners allow you to clean thoroughly in one go through homes with hard floor surfaces, vacuuming *and* mopping as you go. I know—dog hair and paw prints wiped out in one fell swoop. As magical as they sound, it's important to choose your unit wisely. Opt for cleaners that can move quickly over floors (some versions take forever and save you literally no time whatsoever) and leave little or no wet residue. For dog mamas with mostly hard floors these are a great option.

Barrel Pet Hair Vacuum: These suckers are literally designed to suck up animal hair without getting fur stuck in the turbine, and have dedicated air filtration systems to help eliminate dust and dander in the air (a saver for people who suffer from pet allergies!). Coming with an array of cleaning attachments for floor and furniture surfaces, this type of vacuum will help you clean literally every nook and cranny. Suitable for larger spaces, this type of vacuum comes out for a big weekly clean then returns to the cupboard. Easy peasy.

Robotic Pet Vacuum: Now these are a game changer. Why spend your life vacuuming up pet hair when the vacuum can do all the hard work? Robotic vacuums have come a long way since they first hit the market, and while a financial investment, they pay it back in spades. Simply program your vacuum for a scheduled cleanup and return home to a pet-hair-free house.

Depending on your lifestyle, you may find it easier to do one big clean every weekend, quick daily hair patrols to prevent any buildup, or set your robotic vacuum and never look back.

With less hair coming from your dog (due to your amazing brushing and grooming efforts!) you now have a solid base from which to remove any excess pet hair that builds up in your home.

Pro Tip!

To stop shedding at the source, invest in a Dyson groom tool. This adjustable slicker brush attaches to your vacuum hose and removes dead hair directly from your dog. Simply brush, and the collected hair is sucked into your vacuum. It takes a bit of practice for your dog to get used to it, but once you get the hang of it, the Dyson groom tool cuts your grooming and cleaning time in half!

Be Prepared for Quick Cleanups

The last piece of the pet hair puzzle is all about those pesky flyaways that seem to turn up in the most random of places. I mean, I once found a dog hair inside a dry cleaning bag. Yes, it was my dog's hair, and yes, that dry cleaning bag was fresh straight from the cleaners. I swear dog hair has magical powers to get anywhere and everywhere.

To help you stay pet-hair free, here's what you need to eliminate those final furry hairs:

Vinegar: Adding half a cup of white distilled vinegar to your rinse cycle helps prevent pet hair from clinging to clothes and sheets.

Lint Rollers: Unless you want to spend your days picking dog hairs off your clothes, you need a lint roller in your life. While some people like to use rolls of Scotch tape, a quality lint roller is inexpensive and worth its weight in gold. It picks up little bits that vacuums can't. I like to keep a large one at home for clothes, pillows, and soft furnishings; and then a smaller version in the car or my purse for last-minute touch-ups.

Dishwasher Gloves: An oldie but a goodie. This last-minute, everyday fail-safe for pet hair involves nothing more than popping on a set of rubber dishwashing gloves and sweeping your hand over the area you need to "defuzz." It's a quick, cheap, and effective hack for small cleanups when you don't have a lint roller.

Handy Hint

Sprinkling my Doggy Deodorizer (see page 51) over carpets and upholstery before you vacuum loosens hair and acts as an odor neutralizer and room freshener.

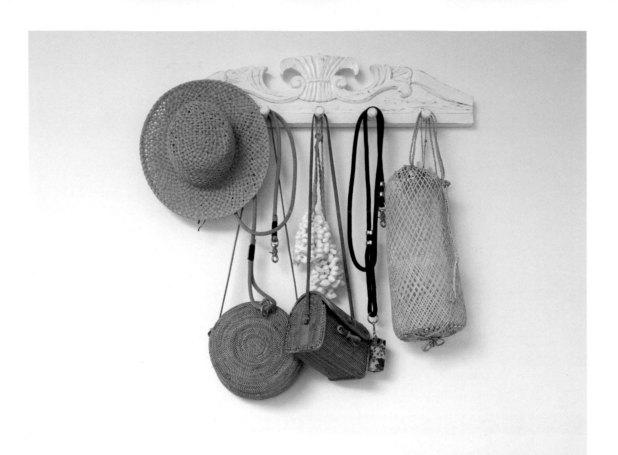

Organizing with Pets

When people first get to know me, they soon learn I have two great loves in my life—dogs and organization (*sorry, family*). The problem with having these two great loves? Well, they make as good a combination as mashed potatoes and chocolate. Great on their own, but together? Not so much. You see, dogs care very little about organization. Their world is a tornado of dirt, hair, and paw prints.

Well, dog mamas, it's time to channel Marie Kondo and get your house in order. Top Tip: Don't ask your dog if items "spark joy" . . . you'll be keeping everything, and your friends will be signing you up for an episode of *Hoarders* in no time.

Clean Out & Declutter

Go through your dog's belongings, such as toys, food dishes, collars, accessories, and blankets, then sort all items into four piles: keep, clean/repair, donate, trash.

- **Keep** means an item that your dog still uses weekly (or seasonally—hello humiliating holiday reindeer antlers), that remains in good condition.
- **Clean/Repair** is for items that your dog still uses, but may need to be washed (i.e., old bedding, collars, etc.) or repaired (such as toys that can be sewn back together) before they can be returned to daily use.
- **Donate** stands for items that your dog no longer uses but remain in good condition—think old toys, extra leashes, or blankets that a shelter dog would *love* to receive. There is nothing quite like giving a bunch of toys to a rescue shelter. Head there at Christmastime and you totally feel like Santa Claus!
- **Trash** is just that—old items that cannot be repaired and need to be thrown out or recycled. Remember that broken toys or faulty leashes can be harmful to your dog's health, so this is no time to be sentimental.

Be ruthless and act quickly. Don't drag this process out, or you'll be left sitting on your living room floor surrounded by junk that seems impossible to throw away. Once you have your piles, action all four, meaning at the end of your day you should be left with one pile of "Keep" items and one pile of repaired and freshly washed items that can join them.

Handy Hints

1. Create a playlist to see you through the task. Put on your favorite motivational songs and also set a time limit to your list. That way when you're reaching the final songs you have to work quickly to finish on time!

2. Really struggling over whether to keep or donate an item? Create a fifth option—grab a small storage box and use it for items that you are unsure about discarding. If you go back to retrieve your item after six months you can keep it, if not, toss it.

3. You can use this same sorting method for your own sheets, towels, and other linens—keeping in mind that dog shelters often use old towels and sheets for dog bedding and kindly accept donations.

Doggo Storage Solutions

Now that you have washed and repaired all of your dog's items that you want to keep, it's time to organize them.

Excluding your pet's bedding, get every single dog product from all over your home and sort into four piles:

- EAT. Dry food, wet food, treats, etc.
- PLAY. Toys, treat balls, etc.
- GROOM. Shampoos, brushes, deodorizers, etc. and VET. Medication, flea and tick treatments, etc.
- WALK. Collars, leashes, harnesses, waste bags, etc. and WEAR. Jumpers, bandanas, accessories, etc.

EAT

Nothing says ugly and boring like dog food storage. Yet whether you're storing dry dog food, wet food, or treats, there are just three easy steps to simple, yet ridiculously good looking, pet food storage.

DOG FOOD STORAGE SOLUTION: DRY FOOD

For most people, kibble forms the main part of their pet's diet, so of course it gets number one billing when we're talking about storage. And the biggest obstacle to overcome here? The sheer bulkiness of those bags! Even the smaller bags prove hard to store. Over the years, I've tried a number of storage solutions for dry food, and my current fave is breaking it down into two parts:

PRO TIPS FOR DRY PET FOOD STORAGE

- Always keep in an airtight container.
- Store out of direct sunlight, in a cool, dry place away from temperature extremes.
- Dog-proof access to your food.
- Discard any food past the use-by date.
- Always keep the bag and bar code in case of recalls.

PART 1—Everyday Food

For a simple everyday solution, I use a lightweight, transparent, airtight container with a handle that fits neatly into my pantry. Each week I transfer at least seven days' worth of kibble into this container—which means easy access at dinnertime. It genuinely saves *so. much. time.* And with a cute label, it blends seamlessly into a stylish pantry layout.

PART 2—Long-Term Storage

(Or as I call it—the rest of the bag!) Now, the important thing to know here is pet food companies spend a lot of money on designing pet food bags to keep the food fresh. By keeping the kibble in the bag it comes in, it stays fresh and tasty for your dog. You also have the bag to refer to for expiry dates, and if there are ever any pet food recalls.

Once you've poured your weekly kibble into your smaller container, roll your bag tightly, shut and seal with a heavy-duty clip (remember to keep it airtight—air leads to moisture, mold, and bacteria), and pop it at the bottom of your pantry or tucked away in another storage container. I choose to store all my dry dog food in the pantry as it's cool, dry, and out of direct sunlight. While a lot of dog owners leave their dog food in the garage, laundry, or shed, the extreme temperatures in these areas don't make them ideal for pet food storage.

DOG FOOD STORAGE SOLUTION: TREATS

Hands up—who buys pet treats, opens them, and then leaves them lying around the kitchen? Yep, I totally used to do that too. But not anymore. Sister got herself some dedicated treat jars. What's to love about them?

They're inexpensive. Whether you buy dollar store versions, or recycle old honey and coffee jars, treat jars leave you with change in your pocket.

Their airtight seals keep the treats smelling and tasting fresh to your furry friend. Because some treats can be stored for more than a week, glass is preferable over long-term plastic storage. However if you use plastic, opt for BPA-free versions.

Handy Hint

Sick of cleaning up drool, food scraps, and dribbled water near your dog's bowls? Pop a large tablemat or rimmed tray under their bowls to catch the mess. Opt for versions that are easy to wipe down for simple cleaning.

DOG FOOD STORAGE SOLUTION: WET FOOD

When it comes to wet food, whether you prefer store-bought or homemade pet food, both require safe storage. In my experience I've found the easiest and safest way is using reusable containers and washi tape labels. Why are they great?

Once opened, canned pet food ideally should not be left in the can. It's not good for the other contents in your fridge, or the quality of the pet food inside. Plus apparently dog food left in the can doesn't taste too good. I have no idea who tested out that theory, but thank them for their service.

Reusable containers allow the portions of a can or a homemade batch of food to be divided into meal portions and frozen/microwaved where necessary. Again glass is ideal, but BPA-free, microwave friendly plastic works just as well.

Washi tape labels are a simple, stylish, and cheap way to display use-by dates.

MAKE YOUR OWN WET DOG FOOD STORAGE

You'll Need:
Reusable containers, washi tape.

Method:
1. Simply divide the full amount of wet food into meal portions and place into containers. I tend to pop them into daily portions as they can be heated separately that way and don't need to be spooned out twice.
2. Attach a snippet of washi tape and write on the use-by date.
3. Once a meal is eaten, simply remove the tape, wash the container, and you're ready to start again.

PLAY

Just like toddlers, dogs leave their toys everywhere, driving everyone else slowly insane. But this simple hack solves that problem in no time.

Split your dog's toys into two separate toy boxes—one larger storage box that is kept out of the dog's reach, and one smaller one placed in the living area. A simple woven (easily cleaned) or felt (easily washed) basket that blends into its surroundings works perfectly.

Fill the smaller box with 3–4 toys only, and leave the remainder in the large one. Then every week or so rotate the toys in the small toy box. This will ensure the toys are enjoyed evenly by your dog and they never become bored with what's on offer!

Why do I love this method?

Fewer toys to pick up daily = More time for Facebook stalking (or trips to the dog park . . . yes, let's do that instead).

Your dog focuses on the few toys out rather than playing with every single toy for five seconds each and moving on.

The rotation of toys allows you the opportunity to see if any toys need mending or need to be tossed. Squeakers and stuffing within pet toys can be harmful to your pets, so it's good to keep a close eye on the toys' condition.

No more toys are forgotten and lost to the elements outside. If you've ever found a soggy, dirt-riddled dog toy in your backyard you know what I'm talking about.

GROOM & VET

Depending on your dog's grooming and health needs, this section can be simple or expansive.

While these items need to be easily accessible (for daily brushing, medication, etc.), it's also important they are safely stored.

For this reason, these items may be best kept in various places around your home:

Grooming tools can be stored in your dog's dedicated cupboard and accessed monthly or as needed.

Hang your dog's brush on a hook next to their walking leash—this serves as a great reminder to give them a daily brush!

Just like our own medications, dog medications need to be kept in a cool, dry place away from dogs and small children.

For supplements and daily meds, store these safely next to your dog's dry food to ensure they're not forgotten.

Pro Tip!

If you find a toy that you use consistently and your dog *loves*, consider buying another one to keep for the future when the original becomes worn out. Only do this if you adore it, otherwise you're just adding to clutter. But if you really do, this means you have it on hand even if the item gets discontinued or the design altered.

WALK & WEAR

Now this storage can be as simple or as extravagant as your dog. Are you a minimalist with one collar and leash? Or is your pup a burgeoning Insta star with a whole doggo wardrobe filled with favorite outfits? (If this is you, see page 115 for even more fashion and storage tips from Instagram sensation Honey I Dressed the Pug.)

If you're finding yourself the dog mama of the latter, you may need more space, but inherently the concept is the same.

Clean out a cupboard (or drawer) dedicated to your dog and put away the items section by section.

Wrap dog leashes and collars in a circular motion to pack away neatly and avoid tangles. This results in a much nicer looking display that ensures you always know what items you have to choose from and nothing gets lost.

For clothes, the Marie Kondo method of folding and storing vertically is a space saver and allows you to see all items at a glance.

For daily use items, such as your dog's walking leash, consider hanging on a hook by the door for easy access.

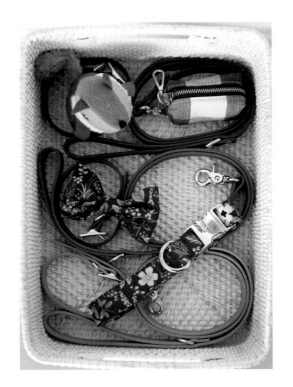

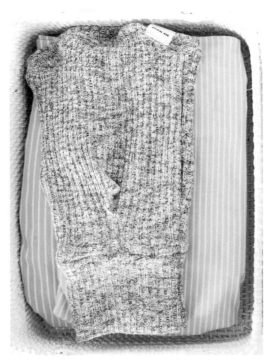

Safety First!

Always be sure that any paint or glue is dry before allowing your dog to interact with their new and improved toy basket. Ensure there are no loose particles that could be a choking hazard for your pup and always remove any trim that become frayed or loose.

DIY: Toy Baskets

While there are hundreds of cute storage baskets on the market these days, not everyone wants to spend a fortune on a stylish toy bin that may or may not get chewed on and covered in drool.

   These budget-friendly baskets are the perfect way to store your dog's favorite toys while still blending in seamlessly to your home decor. Simply transform a dollar store basket into anything you want!

You'll Need:

- Standard dollar-store woven basket
- Paintbrush
- Nontoxic craft paint in your chosen colors
- Painters tape/stencils
- Scissors
- Hot glue gun
- Variety of ribbons, trim, yarn, etc.

Design Ideas:

Paint: Here you can copy designer baskets you've seen, paint your basket to match your decor, or stencil in your favourite pattern or phrase. Whether you love pastels, metallic, monochrome . . . get creative to create a look you love.

Trim: Nothing turns a plain basket into a cute storage solution quicker than this. Ribbon, twine, rope, sequins, pom-poms, and more . . . whether you're going for a boho luxe vibe or a traditional Hamptons feel, these little extras can make your toy basket a statement piece. Trims can be adhered with a hot glue gun on the handles, sides, and edges of the basket—time to get creative!

Cleaning with Dogs: Your Ultimate Guide

Muddy paw prints, nose smudges, pet hair, and more—living with a dog can be messy! But it doesn't have to be. This step-by-step guide to cleaning with pets will allow you and your pooch to enjoy a clean home every day.

Daily: The 15-Minute Clean

These chores can all be done in a 15-minute time frame after dinner and leave your home sparkling for a fresh start the following morning. There's no better way to start the day!

- Pick up all toys and personal items left lying around the house and pack away.
- Do a quick vacuum with a handheld vac over living room floors and high traffic areas. (Or let your robo-vac do it! See page 31.)
- Wash and dry dog bowls (or pop in the dishwasher).
- Wipe down any kitchen surfaces or counters.
- Empty trash and recycling.

WHY SPLIT CLEANING INTO DAILY, WEEKLY, MONTHLY, AND SEASONAL CHORES?

With a clear breakdown of what gets done when, you no longer feel like you're chasing your tail (hello, dog-related pun!) with cleaning. Every cleaning and organizational expert recommends a small amount of cleaning every day combined with bigger jobs done on a regular timetable as the most efficient use of your time.

This way, every morning you get to enjoy a clean home to start with day with, as well as knowing the bigger jobs are covered as needed. There's no cleaning guilt or sweeping the floor five times over in one day. To put it simply: this routine works.

The timing estimates are based on having a one- to two-bedroom home with one dog. Obviously if you have multiple pets, a five-bedroom house, and children thrown in the mix, things may take a bit longer, but the principle is the same.

Weekly: The 1–2 Hour Full Clean

I personally use this method of cleaning every week to get my house in tip-top shape. I follow this particular order of chores as it allows me to maximize the cleaning, with no downtime—getting the job done quicker!

If you can, I suggest popping your dog outside with their favorite treat ball while you clean. Alternatively have another member of the family take them for a walk (trying to clean your home with a dog in it is like brushing your teeth while eating Oreos).

- Remove all sheets from bedding and pop in the wash.
- Dust tables and surfaces using a microfiber cloth. As you go, sprinkle your Doggy Deodorizer (see page 51) on your carpets and soft furnishings to be vacuumed up later.
- Rotate your dog's toys in their toy box (see page 40 for details).
- Clean your kitchen, wiping down surfaces, sinks, and appliances. Replenish dog food supplies including treats and food (see page 36 for dog food storage tips).
- Clean any glass surfaces free of nose smudges and paw prints.
- Vacuum all rooms throughout the house, including soft furnishings and your dog's bed. Use a lint roller to pick up any stray pet hairs on upholstery.
- Mop all hard surfaces (such as floorboards, tiles)—it's a good idea to leave this for last so it has time to dry.
- Clean your bathroom, wiping down surfaces and sinks. Clean toilet, shower, and bath. Reward yourself with a shower at the end and you're ready to start your day! Go get yourself some avocado toast, dog mama.

Monthly: 1–2 Hour Deep Clean

This easy cleaning and organization session will set you up for the month ahead. Just add these chores to your regular weekly clean once a month.

- Wash all dog bedding, apparel, fabric harnesses, leashes, and toys. Most are machine washable these days but always check the label. For hard toys such as Kongs, hand wash and drip dry.
- Treat any leather collars and leashes with a suitable conditioner.
- Spot clean any marks on walls or furnishings.
- Fully wash and rinse treat jars and all food containers.
- Clean out any dog items from the interior of your car and wash any throws you use to protect the upholstery.
- Take stock of your pet supplies, and order any waste bags, grooming tools, or medication your dog needs.

Handy Hint

Pop on your favorite face and hair masks while cleaning your bathroom. In the time it takes you to clean, your treatments will be done!

Pro Tip!

A doggy towel or doormat at your back door will help prevent muddy paw prints coming into your house!

Seasonal Spring Clean

Depending on your dog and lifestyle you may not need to do all of these steps. Consider which ones you need, those you don't, and order yourself some Uber Eats at the end to reward yourself!

- Spring clean your dog's things (see Organizing with Pets on page 35).
- Clean out all food and medications and ensure they are within their use-by dates. Discard any expired food or medication.
- Steam clean carpets and furniture.
- Wash all windows and glass doors, inside and out.
- Diarize your dog's medical appointments, vaccinations, and grooming bookings as needed.

What about Outside Areas?

For people with dogs that spend a lot of time outside, maintaining your outdoor areas is a must. The great thing is this area can use the daily, weekly, monthly, and seasonal breakdown just like the inside.

Daily
- Pick up any dog waste and dispose (or clean out dog potty).
- Return any toys left outside back to toy box.

Weekly
- Mow lawns and weed as required.
- Sweep outdoor balconies, paths, and decks.
- Wipe down any outdoor furniture.
- Clean out any outdoor doghouses or bedding—sweep away any spiderwebs and debris.

Monthly
- Fertilize grass (dogs can be tough on delicate grass, so this is a must!).

Seasonal
- Clean exterior floors, paths, and doghouse with a high-pressure hose.
- Fill any damaged areas from scratching and apply new sealant/paint.
- Patch any grass that needs to be repaired.

DIY: All-Natural Doggy Deodorizer

This all-natural mix not only freshens up the air in a room, it's great at loosening built-up fur, absorbing excess moisture, and trapping unpleasant smells (three things that come hand in hand with having a dog!) Just sprinkle, vac, and enjoy!

You'll Need:

- 1 clean, empty medium-sized jar
- Baking soda (enough to fill the jar)
- 3–5 Drops essential oil (lavender, rosemary, and peppermint all smell great and are natural flea repellants)

Method:

1. Fill the jar with baking soda, add your oil drops, and shake to combine.
2. (Optional) I punched holes in the lid of my jar for easy sprinkling and even distribution.

How to Use:

Sprinkle on carpets, furnishings, dog beds, and toys, and leave for up to 30 minutes (ensure your dog has no access to this space during that time). Follow up with a thorough vacuum.

Apartment Living
with
Stephanie Sterjovski Jolly

Stephanie Sterjovski Jolly is a lifestyle blogger, shop owner (*For Such A Time Shop*), and self-proclaimed crazy dog lady! Her heart's purpose is to encourage women to live an intentional, grace-filled lifestyle through content that breathes life, hope, and inspiration. Stephanie currently lives in Toronto, Canada, with her husband Neal Jolly and their Parson Jack Russell Terrier, Lucy Jolly.

How does your dog make your house a home?
Lucy is the energy in our home! She's so playful and silly—a typical Jack Russell Terrier. She definitely sets the temperature, and it is so hard not to laugh when she is around. She has the most ridiculous personality!

Coming through the door to her jumping up for a lick on our face, hanging out on the couch with her snuggled right against you in the blankets, cooking in the kitchen while she patiently plants herself by your feet—she's in this place in every way!

@stephsterjovski
www.stephaniesterjovski.com

What are your top styling and practical tips for living in an apartment or small space with a dog?

When we went for training Lucy, a defiant, dominant, highly energetic Jack Russell Terrier, our instructor said something that really stuck with us.

Your home is a place for your dog to rest.

We stimulate her in different ways and activities outside of our condo, but when she is here, we want her to feel like she can just relax and rest. We've created little pockets for her to take an afternoon nap: a cave-like bed, blankets on our couch for her to snuggle in (it also protects our couch) and keeping things pretty minimal to leave some margin for Lucy and us to live without it feeling cluttered. We've kept our condo very open concept with the choices we've made in terms of our couch, round coffee table (leaving space to walk around), and neutral color palette.

Does your dog influence your choice of color scheme and interior decor?

We had a gray love seat and some accent chairs before Lucy and it was a lot more cold, she definitely influenced our decision to get an L-shaped couch so we could all fit on there to snuggle! We subconsciously went with beige because it fit with our neutral style and disguised any of her dog fur!

You have an enviably stylish home. What are five things dog owners can do to make their apartment beautiful AND dog-friendly like yours?

That is so kind!

Our goal is for our home to feel welcoming and cozy.

1. We love a neutral, light color palette. (Could you imagine dark floors or a couch and seeing all that dog fur? This is a better way to disguise it all.)
2. Keep plants and any other fragile details up higher and out of your dog's reach.
3. Use blankets to make your place feel cozy and layered in texture, but also to protect your couch and allow your dog to relax up on there.
4. A cute basket (with a lid) adds a nice touch of decor to your living area, while also storing away your dog's toys in a neat and tidy way.
5. Lastly, just enjoy your life and let your dog feel comfortable. Treating our place like

a museum isn't a fun way to live, we don't really look at anything as "too precious," and we usually purchase home decor that's in an affordable range, so we're not too worried if accidents happen. Life is meant to be lived, and enjoyed, with dogs!

How can other dog mamas make their apartment balconies more pet-friendly?

Lucy loves to sunbathe on the balcony with us, but we never leave her unattended. Especially being a JRT, she can really hop like a kangaroo. She is generally quite nervous as she gets closer to the glass looking out, so thankfully she doesn't test those waters, but we always keep her on a leash and we are close by keeping an eye. We added a little hook so we could attach a long leash and she can still roam around, but she can't get too far! It always makes me sad seeing dogs left out on balconies unattended.

What one item could you, as a dog mama, not live without?

Probably our Dyson vacuum! Jack Russells shed a lot, so this has definitely been our saving grace. I'd say our blankets that I've mentioned a few times too. She's never allowed up on our couch unless we have the protective, cozy blanket, and she actually prefers it that way as well!

Health & Well-Being

Superfoods for Dogs

When the term "Superfood" started being bandied about, I think we all bought into the notion that by eating them that we'd suddenly all have boundless energy, great skin, and silky hair 24/7. That our bowlfuls of quinoa, flaxseed, and avocado would completely balance out getting home at 4:00 a.m. and falling asleep with French fries in our mouth.

We soon learned that glass of goji berry juice could only do so much. . . . And the real case for superfoods lay within incorporating them into a daily diet.

Because, just like when Superman puts his glasses back on, "superfoods" are really just regular old foods that have hidden bonuses within them for optimum health.

So when we're talking about superfoods for dogs, these foods aren't just good for your dog, each superfood has certain properties that help protect, build, and nourish specific elements of your dog's body.

Will they balance out your dog partying til 3:00 a.m. and doing Jager-Bombs? Probably not. In fact, if your dog is doing that right now it might be time to finally stage that intervention and discuss their lifestyle choices (no judgment).

Coconut Oil

The staple of health food nuts everywhere, the "good fats" in coconut mimic the properties of antioxidants and boost vitamin E, promoting tissue health and shiny coats in dogs.

Coconut oil is a great substitute when cooking at home for dogs. It can be used as a butter/fat substitute when making treats, or as a healthy oil alternative when baking.

Quinoa

The darling of the health food circuit, this hard-to-pronounce superfood has brought many of us undone when ordering brunch. Quinn-noah? Quin-nah? For those playing at home, it's pronounced *keen-wah*. Forgiving it for its ridiculous spelling, this superfood is the ultimate addition to a healthy canine diet.

Because quinoa is nutritionally denser than most processed carbohydrates, it makes an excellent rice and grain substitute—brilliant for dogs with allergies. By adding cooked quinoa to a selection of fresh meats and vegetables you have the perfect base for a balanced meal for your pup.

Kale

One of the healthiest things you can do for your dog is to add more green and leafy vegetables to their diet. Kale is a number one choice, being rich in iron, calcium, and vitamins A, C, and K.

Yes, you'll totally sound pretentious buying kale for your dog, but just lie and say it's for your green smoothie or whatever. To include it in your dog's diet you can steam the leaves and add to your dog's dinner, or brush lightly with oil and bake to create doggie chips (that you may want to steal).

Sweet Potato

The cool cousin of the potato family, sweet potato is among the highest vegetables on the nutrition scale—including vitamins A, C, manganese, and iron—which are good for a healthy coat and immune system.

Their high level of fiber also aids in healthy digestion. You can slice and bake them to serve as a snack, or add cooked portions to your dog's dinner.

Carrots

Relegated to school lunch boxes . . . the last to be picked from food platters . . . and boiled within an inch of their lives for Aunty Karen's family dinners . . . the poor carrot hasn't seen the love it deserves over the years.

No, it's not the most exotic or trendy superfood ever to grace our plates. Yet the humble carrot is a long-standing superfood for all pups—packed with beta-carotene, which assists with everything from helping prevent heart disease to healthy eyesight.

They won't help your dog see in the dark, but freshly chopped carrot sticks will keep your dog's stomach fuller until mealtime and keep their teeth healthy.

Another trick with carrots is to use carrot shavings to "bulk up" main meals if you're trying to help your pup lose weight.

Chia

They say good things come in small packages, and chia is no exception. Want a food that has seven times more vitamin C than oranges? Eight times more omega-3 fatty acids than salmon? Six times more fiber than oat bran?

Great for supporting digestion in dogs, chia also contains 20 percent omega-3 ALA—an essential fatty acid that supports brain and heart function. Chia also performs well as an anti-inflammatory agent for skin and irritation problems in senior dogs.

How to use it? You can either sprinkle a small amount on your dog's meal daily, or combine with water to form as gel which acts as the perfect egg replacement in dog treat recipes.

Oily Fish

Has your dog being eyeing your sashimi lately? There's good reason. Oily fish such as salmon and sardines make a perfect addition to any pupper's diet.

These little fishies are an abundant source of omega-3 fats, which support your dog's immune system, as well as maintaining a healthy skin and coat.

Pack them into your pup's diet, either by adding cooked salmon (never raw) or wild-caught sardines in spring water to your dog's dinnertime every so often. Not an everyday food, oily fish are better off served once a week or so for optimum health.

All-Natural Yogurt

Chock-full of calcium and protein, all-natural yogurt is a yummy source of goodness for doggos and a versatile all-round treat. The probiotics (healthy bacteria) in each spoonful also promote a healthy gut and digestion in dogs—which is great for pups with more sensitive tummies.

Just always ensure the yogurt you are using is all natural, and has no sugars or artificial sweeteners (it should say so on the container).

A great way to serve yogurt to your dog is through frozen yogurt treats, or mixed with fresh dog-friendly fruits for a summer treat (see page 63 for more on fruits for dogs).

Got a pupper that has an allergic aversion to dairy? Best to skip the yogurt.

Pumpkin

I guarantee you that nearly every dog owner alive, when faced with a pup with an upset stomach, has been told to give them some mashed pumpkin.

And for good reason. A great choice for pooches with sensitive stomachs, the humble pumpkin is a top source of fiber, which promotes healthy digestion—keeping things "moving" along the digestive tract.

Cooked pumpkin is incredibly versatile; you can add it to your dog's meals or you can mash it and add it to your favorite dog treat recipes.

Flaxseed Oil

Not too long ago you had to go hiking to your nearest health food store to find a bottle of this magic elixir. But thanks to the likes of Gwenyth Paltrow, you can now find this baby in nearly every supermarket (you may not have loved her in *Duets*, but you and your dog owe her for this).

Packed with omega-3 fatty acids, flaxseed oil promotes a healthy skin and coat in dogs with its anti-inflammatory properties proving beneficial for pups with allergies. It's also believed to be beneficial for aging dogs with joint pain or mobility issues.

Simply grab yourself a bottle and pour the recommended dosage over your floofer's food to serve.

Organic Oats

A budget-friendly and bulky source of soluble fiber, oats help support a healthy digestive tract in dogs.

Just like their basic friend the carrot, organic oats are a great way to bulk up treats and food, keeping pups fuller for longer.

They can be served in homemade treats or cooked—but remember your doggo doesn't want any of those added sugars or flavorings you would normally put on your own (but you can still totally sprinkle a little brown sugar for yourself).

Always talk to your vet before making any changes or new additions to your dog's diet.

Fruits for Dogs

We all have that well-meaning friend that encourages us to "eat the rainbow." And we love you Jenna, we really do . . . but do you always have to remind us when we're knee-deep in our morning latte and pick-me-up brownie? (It was the *one* thing getting me through the day.)

But you know what? She has a point. And that point extends to our puppers.

Fresh fruits are an excellent source of vitamins, minerals, and all things good for your doggo. Many can be served fresh, or incorporated into yummy treats and Kong stuffers to keep your pup entertained and nourished.

Yes, you've got to watch the sugar content of fruits—don't let their consumption creep up too high. Yet by adding a few of these yummy delights to your dog's diet, you'll be supporting their health and well-being for years to come. Now go eat that brownie.

Blueberries

Looking for the ultimate lazy dog owner's treat?

Filled with antioxidants known to boost cognitive function in dogs, blueberries are a delicious addition to your pup's diet. A great alternative to bite-sized processed treats, all you need to do is literally wash them and serve.

Feeling like a super dog mom? Blend them with yogurt to make doggie pupsicles, or add them to biscuit mixes to make a healthy snack. Then give yourself a gold star.

Watermelon

Just like the name suggests, watermelons are packed with water, making them an ideal option for rehydrating your pup in hot weather.

Watermelon is a great one to serve fresh in bite-size pieces. Always be sure to remove both the rind and the seeds as they can be toxic and cause intestinal blockages.

Strawberries

Studies have found strawberries contain anti-inflammatory properties that help relieve pain associated with the inflammation of muscles and joints.

A small amount of strawberries in a healthy doggie smoothie or frozen dog treat work well. They also make an excellent topper for doggie birthday cakes. Grab a pint and share with your pup today.

Kiwifruit

Say hello to the green machine. High in potassium, fiber, and vitamin C, kiwis are also a great source of select phytonutrients that are believed to help protect against age-related macular degeneration (vision loss) in dogs.

FRUIT SERVING TIPS

1. Always talk to your vet before introducing new foods to your dog's diet.
2. Where possible, try to buy organic fruits free of high pesticide levels—especially when purchasing strawberries, apples, and pears that are members of the "Dirty Dozen."
3. Always thoroughly wash all produce before serving.
4. Ensure all pits, seeds, and skin (where applicable) are removed.
5. Limit servings to small portions. Treats should never make up more than 10 percent of your dog's diet.

A fresh slice with the skin removed makes an easy and tasty treat you and your dog can share.

Bananas

An excellent source of potassium, vitamins B_6 and C, bananas are as beneficial as they are tasty.

To let your dog go bananas, mash up and spoon into a Kong then freeze, or why not make dog-friendly banana bread or ice cream? These fruits are starchy, so best to limit as a "sometimes food" rather than an everyday treat.

Cranberries

Rich in antioxidants, cranberries can help enhance your dog's immune system and decrease inflammation.

This low-calorie berry packed with vitamin C and fiber packs a punch.

Cranberries can be fed raw, cooked, or dried. They make a fantastic addition to dog treat recipes—adding a pop of flavor to a regular biscuit. Just avoid premade cranberry sauces and juices as they contain additional ingredients and sugars.

Pears

A top source of fiber, folic acid, and vitamins C, K, B1, and B2, pears are a great starter fruit for dogs.

Pears are often recommended as a "hypoallergenic fruit"—if your dog suffers allergies, pears are a great introduction to fruit as they are less likely to produce an adverse response than other fruits.

Pear slices (with the skin on!) make an excellent snack for dogs that love to crunch. Or consider pureeing them and freezing in a Kong for a fun, frozen treat! Always ensure you remove all seeds and pith before serving. Avoid canned versions—this goes for any fruit for dogs.

Raspberries

Raspberries provide a good source of dietary fiber and have a low energy density, allowing your pup to enjoy a sweet treat while leaving them fuller for longer.

Low in sugar in comparison to other dog-safe fruits, they also have anti-inflammatory properties, which make them a great addition to the diets of dogs with joint issues.

It's important to note raspberries DO contain a small amount of xylitol—which is toxic to dogs—about 400 micrograms per gram of raspberry. Therefore it's always best to limit any one serving to no more than half a cup, less for smaller dogs.

A hugely versatile fruit, raspberries can be served fresh, folded into cakes and biscuits, and blended into smoothies and frozen treats.

Pineapple

A sweet treat for your pup, pineapple also contains an enzyme called bromelain that helps dogs break down proteins in their food and aids digestion.

A summer favorite, simply chop into small pieces and freeze for a frosty, fruity treat! Always ensure the prickly outside is completely removed.

DIY: Superfood No-Bake Bliss Balls 3 Ways

No-bake bliss balls are an easy way to add superfoods to your dog's diet without even turning on the oven! They can be fed as stand-alone treats, or make excellent Kong stuffers. Simply make, chill, and you're done!

COCONUT BOMBS

You'll Need:
- ⅓ cup coconut oil
- 2–3 tablespoons organic peanut butter
- 2 cups rolled oats
- ⅓ cup finely shredded coconut

Method:
1. Add coconut oil, peanut butter, and rolled oats to food processor and mix until well combined. If the mixture is too dry or wet simply add extra oats or coconut oil to correct.
2. Scoop out bite-sized pieces with a spoon and roll into little balls.
3. Toss each ball gently in the finely shredded coconut until well coated.
4. Place on a flat tray lined with baking paper, refrigerate for 30 minutes, and serve.

Makes 16 Treat Balls.

BANANA & BEET BITES

You'll Need:

- ¼ cup grated beet
- 1 small banana, peeled and roughly chopped
- 1 cup almond flour
- ⅓ cup finely shredded coconut

Method:

1. Add all ingredients to food processor and mix until smooth.
2. Scoop out bite-sized pieces with a spoon and roll into little balls.
3. *Optional:* Toss each ball gently in some more finely shredded coconut until well coated.
4. Place on a flat tray lined with baking paper, refrigerate for 30 minutes, and serve.

Makes 12–15 Treat Bites.

NO-BAKE PEANUT BUTTER BALLS

You'll Need:

- ½ cup plain organic yogurt
- 1 cup organic peanut butter
- 2½ cups rolled oats

Method:

1. Mix the yogurt and peanut butter until it forms a paste.
2. Add the oats ½ cup at a time ensuring they are fully coated and no dry spots form. You will be left with a heavy mixture.
3. Scoop out bite-sized pieces with a spoon and, using gentle pressure, roll into little balls.
4. Place on a flat tray lined with baking paper, refrigerate for 1 hour, and serve.

Makes 25–30 Treat Balls.

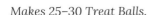

Healthy Herbs for Your Hound

A concentrated source of flavor and nutrition, herbs are not just for humans.

In fact incorporating more herbs into your dog's diet can have a positive effect of increasing the amount of herbs in your own diet. (You and your dog can then decide if you're a house that loves or hates cilantro. There is no in between.)

With so many easy to grow dog-friendly herbs—whether you have a small balcony or a large backyard—you can quickly set up an in-house herb garden to grow these babies at home (no, not that type of herb garden).

Year-round healthy herbs on tap? Yes, please.

Thyme

Packed with vitamins C, A, and K, iron, manganese, calcium, and antioxidants, this little herb is a great immune system booster. Thyme has antiseptic, antispasmodic, and antibacterial properties, making it great for your dog's skin, brain function, and gastrointestinal health.

Serving Ideas:

Add a pinch of thyme leaves to pureed pear and freeze in your dog's Kong for a fruity, frozen treat.

Mint

Fresh mint is a great way to keep your dog's breath smelling sweet, and also has the added effect of helping calm an upset stomach.

Serving Ideas:

Place 3 to 5 mint leaves in fresh water and allow to infuse for one hour. Serve your dog the infused water (minus the leaves) for a refreshing summer drink.

Add a small handful of freshly chopped mint to your favourite dog biscuit recipe to create fresh breath cookies.

Rosemary

Love to add rosemary to your roasted veggies? Well, it's time to add it to your dog's diet too! Packed with iron and calcium, rosemary is also a natural antioxidant.

Serving Ideas:

Sprinkle some freshly chopped rosemary on wafer-thin slices of pumpkin and sweet potato. Toss with coconut oil and roast in the oven for a delectable snack.

Basil

An easy herb to grow in your garden, basil has anti-inflammatory and antibacterial properties, which promote gut, joint, and cardiovascular health in dogs.

Serving Ideas:

Sprinkle some freshly chopped basil on roasted chickpeas and toss with coconut oil.

Add a small amount of finely chopped basil to your dog's wet food every so often.

Parsley

It's not just for decoration! Just like us, dogs benefit from the breath-freshening properties of parsley. As an added bonus, it also is a great source of antioxidants, vitamins C, K, B, and iron. Doggie kisses, anyone?

Serving Ideas:

Add freshly chopped parsley to your dog's wet food every so often.

Add finely chopped parsley to doggie cupcakes, biscuits, and baked goods as a breath freshener.

Ginger

Studies have shown fresh ginger has been known to reduce inflammation and upset stomachs in dogs, making it a great ingredient for dogs with allergies.

Serving Ideas:

Doggie Gingerbread Men! These delicious holiday dog biscuits make a great gift for dog lovers.

Healthy Snack Alternatives

"Just give me my pup, my Netflix, and my snacks."
—Dog Mamas, everywhere.

Let's be honest, up there with true love, a beautiful home, and a successful career . . . one of life's greatest joys is snacks. You know it. I know it. And your dog knows it.

Snacks can come as the delicious but not-so-good-for-us (hello 9:00 p.m. ice cream binges) and the wow-I-feel-good-for-eating-that (that bliss ball you ate once thinking it was chocolate). And pupper snacks are just the same.

By swapping out some of the heavily processed store-bought treats for healthier alternatives, your dog's well-being will skyrocket.

And, more importantly with most of these snacks being totally human friendly, for once you can steal your dog's food instead of it being the other way around.

Store-Bought Buy: Processed dental sticks
Healthy Snack to Try: Apple slices
A pup with healthy teeth and gums can avoid a number of medical issues, especially as they grow older.

While a dental stick can be a handy chew that keeps your dog busy while you head off to work, there is some doubt in the pet industry about their overall effectiveness. Formulated to be a tasty treat that also helps scrape tartar from your dog's teeth, the highly processed ingredients and gummy materials used to hold the product together can actually sometimes stick to your dog's teeth, undoing much of its good work.

A more budget-friendly, nourishing alternative is the humble apple. A healthy source of vitamin A, C, and phytonutrients (a fancy word for natural chemicals found in plants), fresh apple slices can also help clean your dog's teeth while chewing.

Dogs love them served fresh with the skin on (to retain all those healthy chemicals)—just be sure to always remove any seeds, as they are toxic.

Store-Bought Buy: Canned fillers
Healthy Snack to Try: Natural peanut butter
In the popular era of Kongs and other treat toys ruling the market, along came canned fillers to fill them with. Stuff your treat ball with these fillers and keep your dog occupied for hours—what could be better than that?

Yet, while these canned fillers are often flavored with natural-sounding ingredients (i.e., liver) they are heavily processed to ensure they have a long supermarket shelf life.

Luckily enough there are a myriad of healthy dog treat alternatives to pop in your dog's treat ball and keep them occupied. One easy, delicious favourite is natural peanut butter.

A tasty source of protein, natural peanut butter is used to build and repair muscle tissue, while being filled with "good fats" that support a healthy cardiovascular system. Always ensure you choose a natural peanut butter that does not contain xylitol, which is toxic to dogs.

Other great treat ball options include freshly cooked chicken (no bones/fat) pieces, mashed pumpkin, or you can even make a frozen "pupsicle" treat by filling it with natural yogurt and berries.

Store-Bought Buy: "Meaty" training bites
Healthy Snack to Try: Chicken or kangaroo pieces

When training your dog, it's great to have bite-sized treats to encourage and reward them. Any good trainer will tell you, you're only as good as the treats you carry.

The trouble with so many of the supermarket training treat brands is the ingredients are often high in processed fillers and preservatives while being low in nutritional value.

The best healthy alternative is to replace these treats with fresh produce. Options such a fresh-cooked chicken pieces work the best as they still retain a tasty smell that demands your dog's attention. Kangaroo is another option. While it's harder to find in the grocery store, kangaroo has a strong, enticing scent that helps train even the trickiest pooches!

Simply pop these meat treats in a zip-top bag and store them in a cool spot to keep them fresh for that day's training. Remember, with rich treats like these, a little goes a long way. Keep treats small and to a minimum to avoid upset tummies.

10 UNSAFE SNACK FOODS FOR DOGS

1. Avocado
2. Candy (all varieties)
3. Cherries
4. Chewing gum
5. Chocolate (all variations)
6. Citrus fruits
7. Grapes
8. Macadamia nuts
9. Mushrooms
10. Raisins

Store-Bought Buy: Mini dog biscuits
Healthy Snack to Try: Air-popped popcorn and roasted chickpeas

Nothing says "dog treat" like a biscuit in the shape of a bone. They're cute and they remind us of the yummy biscuits and cookies we love to eat ourselves. Yet, for a lot of dogs, the ingredients used to make these store-bought dog biscuits can cause allergies. Additionally, dogs can wolf down these biscuits in a matter of seconds—meaning one too many of these biscuits and their waistline might start expanding.

Two natural, healthy alternatives—that you totally can share as well—are air-popped popcorn and roasted chickpeas.

A tasty, crunchy snack, air popped popcorn gives your dog a yummy treat without the preservatives and calories of store-bought treats (always ensure you remove any un-popped kernels before serving).

High in fiber and protein, chickpeas make another nourishing alternative. If your dog loves chewy treats, simply serve your cooked chickpeas plain. If they like a bit of crunch, roast them in the oven for a hearty snack.

Store-Bought Buy: Processed dog jerky and rawhides

Healthy Snack to Try: Baked chicken strips
Dogs love to chew, and highly processed dog jerky and treat strips are a staple in every supermarket pet food aisle. However as the years go by more and more dog owners come to realize they may not be as nourishing as they seem. Not only do many of these processed jerky or treat strips have low nutritional content, often the origin of the treat is unknown.

Once a top choice, rawhide dog treats have lessened in popularity over the years due to health scares involving cross-contamination and the risk of dogs choking or experiencing digestive blockages from a chewed rawhide.

For a safe and healthy alternative, you can easily bake your own dog treat strips at home.

AT HOME RECIPE: HEALTHY CHICKEN STRIPS

You'll Need:
1 chicken breast, slightly thawed
Note: *It is recommended to freeze meat for at least 1 week prior to turning them into chews. This helps kill any parasites in the meat.*

Method:
1. Preheat oven to 100°C / 210°F—select "Vent Bake" on your oven if you have that option. Line a flat baking tray with baking paper.
2. Slice the chicken breast into thin strips. Having your chicken only slightly thawed makes it easier for you to cut into the strips.
3. Place the chicken strips on your prepared baking tray, and bake for 3 hours. (If your oven doesn't have a "vent bake" option, after about 1½ hours you can open the oven door slightly and leave ajar to decrease moisture. Only do this if the environment is safe to do so. Do not leave your oven unattended.)
4. Increase the temperature to 150°C / 300°F and blast for 3 minutes at that temperature to kill any surface pathogens—this makes the treats safe for you to handle.
5. Remove from oven, allow to cool on tray for 10 minutes, and then transfer to cooling racks.
6. Cover with a dish towel and dry overnight at room temperature.

Makes approximately 12 Chicken Strips.

Grooming Like a Boss

After years of painstaking research, experts from around the globe revealed their top secret for dog grooming: take your dog to a groomer and let someone else do it.

But in reality, groomer or no groomer, the task of caring for your dog's everyday grooming comes down to you. Unless you live with a dog groomer, that is.

From brushing to washing, floofing to fluffing, and everything in between, a well-groomed dog is a healthy, happy dog.

And once you have the right tools and know what you're doing, it's actually all very easy.

What Type of Coat Is Your Pup?

Ever done one of those quizzes to find out whether your skin was dry or oily, so you knew what products to use in the intricate seventeen-step program they recommended? (And then you totally bought all the products because you were intimidated by the lady at the makeup counter?)

Well, just like those quizzes, before you start grooming your dog you need to know what sort of coat they have.

Smooth Coat

Short, smooth, shiny hair, close to the body.

Such as: Greyhound, Staffordshire Terrier, Boston Terrier

Requires the least amount of grooming—brush at least once a week with a bristle or pin brush.

Short Coat

Short hair close to the body that is more textured.

Such as: Labrador Retriever, Beagle, Pug

Brush a few times a week with a bristle or pin brush.

Long Coat

Continuously growing coats that can be silky or coarse.

Such as: Old English Sheepdog, Maltese, Shih Tzu

Brushing with a pin brush and comb required at least three times a week. For dogs that experience tangles, consider investing in a detangler spray.

Curly Coat

Soft, curly, or wavy coat that are considered non-shedding.

Such as: Poodle, Bichon Frise

Brush with a soft slicker brush at least three times a week to prevent tangles and matting.

Wire Coat

Soft, dense undercoat and wiry overcoat.

Such as: Schnauzer, Airedale Terrier

Brush daily with a slicker brush, and once or twice a week with an undercoat rake to thin the wiry undercoat.

Double Coat

Harsh outer guard coat with thick, soft undercoat.

Such as: Malamute, Husky, Corgi, Shiba Inu

During their shedding season brush daily, less in non-shedding season. Use an undercoat rake or de-shedding tool for the thick undercoat, and a slicker brush for the top coat followed by a gentle comb.

Silky Coat

Short coat around the face and front of body. Long, silky coat on the undercarriage and tail.

Such as: Cocker Spaniel, Irish Setter

Brush three or four times a week with a slicker brush and double comb, ensuring the longer sections are free from tangles and matting. Pay close attention to around and behind their ears.

Combination Coat

Combination of a smooth and silky coat. Short around the face, front body, and legs. Longer on the undercarriage, rear legs, and tail.

Such as: Golden Retriever, Australian Shepherd, Border Collie

Brush at least four times a week with a slicker brush and double comb. Pay attention to feathering around the ears, tail, and legs.

Heavy Coat

Thick, dense coat with some short, smooth hair.

Such as: Samoyed, Pomeranian, Collie

Brush four to seven times a week—starting with a double comb to separate hairs and check for mats, followed by a slicker brush.

Hairless Coat

Hair-free, with some having tufts on head, legs, or tail.

Such as: Chinese Crested Dog

Brush tufts as required to prevent tangling.

Pro Tip!

Got a new pup? Introduce them to brushing and baths early. Dogs that experience grooming in the critical period between three and seventeen weeks of age are less likely to show signs of stress and anxiety with it in later life. Get them used to the bath, nail clippers, brushing, and generally having their bodies, paws, ears, and extremities handled.

If you plan to use a professional groomer, take your pup there during this time as well. Your groomer can give them pats and treats, and your pup will then forever more see trips to the groomer as a "treat yo' self" kind of day.

Groomer's Tool Kit

Slicker brush

Featuring thin wire bristles sitting on a slightly curved or flat base, this type of brush works with all coat types. Great for curly coats and dogs that shed a lot, it removes loose fur and detangles knots. Opt for versions with angled or protective nub bristles to prevent damage to your doggo's skin.

Pin brush

Similar to the slicker brush, but with wider spaced wire pins tipped with plastic or rubber ends. It's made for silkier coat types and is great for removing tangles in dogs with longer fur.

Bristle brush

The ideal finishing brush for all coat types. Bristle brushes smooth the hair and spread healthy skin oils through the coat (giving that glossy shine!) Stiffer bristle brushes are great for puppers with short or wiry coats, while short bristles are perfect for smooth-coated dogs.

Undercoat rake

The ultimate tools for shedding dogs, undercoat rakes remove loose undercoat fur easily and prevents painful matting. Always be gentle with undercoat rakes as their pins could hurt your dog if pressed too hard.

PRO TIPS FOR BRUSHING

1. Always, always be gentle. Rough brushing can irritate and damage the skin.
2. If your dog hates brushing, start with just a few strokes building up to a full brush. The more treats offered, the better!
3. Use your free hand to part your dog's hair against the grain and then make brush strokes in the direction of the hair growth. This allows you to check your dog's skin (for fleas, growths, etc.) and brush the full coat thoroughly.
4. Always pay close attention to hair around the eyes, ears, nose, and face to ensure there are no accidents.
5. If your dog has a large section of matted hair, consider taking them to a professional to remove it to avoid damage to your dog's skin.
6. Try to make brushing a calm, enjoyable experience and keep grooming sessions short. Reward your dog with a treat at the end and reward yourself with a glass of wine!

Double comb

The wider teeth on this comb minimize tangles and remove dirt and debris from the fur. The finer teeth help remove loose fur, deep cleaning the coat. Ideal for all medium to longhaired coats.

Rubber massage brushes (such as the Kong Zoom Groom)

A great starter brush, the rubber teeth simultaneously remove dead hair while stimulating capillaries to promote blood and oil flow for a healthier skin and coat. Ideal for short coats, or used wet during your dog's bath.

No More Tears: How to Wash Your Dog

All dogs need to be bathed regularly. They'll hate me telling you this, but it's true.

Depending on your dog's coat, lifestyle, and general ability to get covered in dirt you'll need to wash your dog every four to eight weeks. Anything less than three weeks can dry out your dog's skin and strip your dog's hair of natural oils that protect it from damage and keep it silky and shiny.

This can be done at a reputable groomer, but if you have a sensitive dog,* would prefer to do it yourself, or just want to blow that cash

_____

* Or like me was politely asked to never to return to the groomer because all seventy-five pounds of my golden retriever kept jumping and rolling around to avoid the water. "He's always welcome back for pats and hugs!" they said.

on a pampering session for yourself—here's what to do.

Important note: Before you even attempt to bathe your dog, make sure they are comfortable with water and have positive associations with the spot you wash them in. If this means building them up day by day until they're comfortable sitting in the laundry tub being fed treats like an Egyptian goddess, that's what you do.

1. Start

Pick a dedicated spot to wash your dog—most people opt for the laundry or mudroom, bathroom, or backyard. Ensure you have all the materials you need on hand—shampoo, conditioner, hose attachment for rinsing, towels, washcloths, and treats. Make sure everything is within reach, because once bath time starts you're not going to want to have to leave your dog alone for any period of time (unless you enjoy your home being covered in muddy paw prints, that is). Given the opportunity, your dog can and will escape.

2. Brush

Brush your dog thoroughly before their bath. This removes any tangles or excess fur (and will save your sink from getting clogged—you're welcome).

3. Wet

If washing in a tub, place a rubber mat on the base to prevent your dog from slipping.

Handy Hint

Secret Dog Hack #312: To distract an anxious dog that doesn't like baths, try smearing bits of peanut butter over the tub. This allows your pooch to be distracted licking up the treat while you get on with the job at hand. Yes, it's a bit gross and you have to clean it up later, but thousands of dog owners swear by it.

Don't fill the tub with water (unless you just want everyone and everything to be covered in water at the end). Instead place your dog in the bath and use a hose attachment to wet your dog's hair all the way down to the skin. Work from the chest area down the back, sides, legs, and undercarriage until you reach the tail. Keep the water lukewarm and on low pressure to ensure your pupper is comfortable at all times. Use a washcloth to wet your dog's face and ears, being careful not to get water in their eyes or ears.

4. Wash

Once your doggo is thoroughly wet, apply a small, diluted amount of shampoo. Start at the chest and massage gently through the coat to the tail. Don't forget your dog's legs and feet. Think back to all the scalp massages you've enjoyed at the hairdressers and try to replicate that bliss for your pup.

Pro Tip!

Always use a pet-friendly hypoallergenic shampoo specific for your dog's coat and skin type—and don't forget to patch test on your dog before trying a new brand.

5. Rinse

Using your hose attachment, gently rinse out the shampoo. Use your fingers or a rubber massage brush to ensure all traces are thoroughly rinsed throughout the coat until the water runs clear. Double-check your dog's armpits, under their legs, chest, and bottom—leftover suds can cause skin irritation.

Handy Hint

Just like us, dogs can benefit from two washes. Wash, rinse, and repeat to keep your dog cleaner for longer.

6. Shine

Next up, conditioner. This is a controversial step, as some professional groomers claim conditioners are not needed. However if you find your dog's coat responds well to their favorite conditioner, repeat the shampoo steps with conditioner and then rinse thoroughly or leave in according to the product's instructions.

7. Dry

Towel off! Literally everyone's favorite part of dog washing: the end. If you can, opt to sponge off the excess water with absorbent towels then leave your pooch to air dry naturally. Pay particular attention to ensuring your dog's ears and skin folds are dry. Just like us, rubbing vigorously with towels or using hot hairdryers can damage the hair. If you prefer to blow dry, either use a specific dog-safe dryer or ensure your hairdryer is on the lowest setting—keep your hand near the airflow to monitor the temperature and protect your dog from getting too hot.

Pampered Extras

Nails

Many dogs wear down their nails through regular walking, however if they are getting too long, they need to be trimmed with a dog nail clipper.

Cut to the curve of each nail, well below the blood vessel (the pinkish area on transparent nails) and just trim a small amount off the tip. Like at home eyebrow waxing, nail trimming is sometimes best left to the professionals—if you're unsure, ask your vet or groomer to take charge.

Teeth

Here you can fall into one of three camps:

- Those who believe chew toys, bones, and vet checkups alone keep their dog's teeth healthy.
- Those who brush their dog's teeth every day.
- Those who say they brush their dog's teeth daily, but actually never do.*

Dental disease can lead to much larger (and sometimes life-threatening) health problems

---

* *Me as a pet parent from 2002 to 2005. My secret shame.*

in dogs. Talk to your vet about your dog's dental requirements and make an action plan. If you do want to commit to brushing your dog's teeth, the easiest way to start is to use a finger brush and dog-safe toothpaste.

Trimming

Use blunt-nosed scissors to trim:

- Excess hair around the eye area starting to obscure your dog's eyesight. (Never cut your dog's whiskers at home. Dog's use their whiskers as a sixth sense and cutting them will disorient her.)
- Fur around and under the paw pads to prevent slipping and debris getting trapped.
- Under the chin and jowls if food is getting trapped. (He's not saving it for later.)

Ears

Check your dog's ears on a regular weekly basis and always after swimming.

To clean your dog's ears, use a vet-approved ear cleaner. Squeeze the solution into your dog's ear canal and massage through the base of the ear. Use a clean cotton ball to remove any excess wax from the ear—never use Q-Tips as they can damage the delicate eardrum.

If your dog is shaking their head, scratching, or their ears are red, smelly, or have a discharge, check with your vet—your pooch may have an infection or irritation.

Eyes

Healthy dog eyes are clear and bright. If there are signs of discharge or redness, follow up with your vet.

WHEN TO GROOM AT HOME

- You have the proper tools and equipment to do so.
- You have a safe, suitable space for bathing your dog.
- You feel comfortable handling your dog and using the grooming equipment.
- Your dog enjoys the bonding experience.

WHEN TO GO TO A GROOMER

- You don't want to invest in or store quality grooming equipment.
- You don't have a suitable space for bathing your dog.
- You have the budget for professional grooming.
- You don't feel comfortable handling your dog, or the grooming equipment, on your own.
- You want a specific style or haircut for your dog. (Pro Tip! If you want a specific haircut for your dog, always bring an example photo for your groomer to match.)

DIY: Natural Dog Shampoo & Spray

With all-natural ingredients, this homemade shampoo and cleansing spray combo will keep your dog clean and fresh all year round.

DOG WASH

You'll Need:

- 1 clean, empty bottle (glass is preferable)
- ½ cup warm distilled water
- 3 tablespoons Dr. Bronner's Uncented Pure Castile Soap
- 1 tablespoon Bragg's Organic Apple Cider Vinegar
- 15–20 drops essential oil (lavender, rosemary, and peppermint all smell great and are natural flea repellants)
- ½ teaspoon extra-virgin olive oil

Method:

Simply pour all ingredients into the empty bottle and shake well.

FUR SPRAY

You'll Need:

- 1 clean, empty spray bottle (glass is preferable)
- ½ cup warm distilled water
- 10–12 drops essential oil (lavender, eucalyptus, and sweet marjoram all have calming properties)

Method:

Simply pour all ingredients into the empty bottle and shake well. Always re-shake bottle before spraying.

Your Year-Round At-Home Health Cheat Sheet

Daily
- Brush fur as needed.
- Brush teeth, start once weekly working up to daily routine.
- Medication, vitamins, and health supplements as directed by your vet.

Monthly
- Bath and groom.
- Flea, tick, and worming treatments.
- Nail clipping as needed.
- Fur trimming as needed.
- Check over for new lumps/bumps.
- Check over eyes and ears.
- Monitor weight to keep in the healthy range.

Yearly
- Annual vet checkup.
- Vaccinations.
- Check all registration paperwork is up to date.
- Check your emergency vet details are up to date.
- Check your Pet First Aid Kit (page 90) is up to date and within expiration dates.

Spring & Summer
- Apply dog sunscreen to pink snouts and thinned hair areas.
- Check for hotspots.
- Check for cracked or burnt paws and apply soother.
- Check for fleas and ticks.
- Check for grass seeds.

Fall & Winter
- Protect paws from ice and salt.
- Invest in a winter coat to protect your dog from the elements.
- Reduce baths in severely cold climates.

DIY: Pet First Aid Kit

Channel your inner Doogie Howser and make your own Pet First Aid Kit for pet-related emergencies and accidents.

You'll Need:

- Container: Traditional metal kits have handy compartments for all items, however a sturdy storage box with a snap-lock lid can work just as well
- Cotton pads for cleanup and topical applications
- Gauze for swabbing, padding, or wound cover
- At least two bandages/vet wraps for compression, splints, makeshift muzzle, and dressings
- Adhesive tape for securing pads/bandages
- Q-Tips for topical applications and cleanups
- Blunt-end scissors
- Tweezers
- Antiseptic spray or wipes for small grazes and wounds
- Sterile saline solution for eyes and rinsing
- Disposable gloves
- Sanitizer for your own hands after dealing with wounds
- Pocket flashlight

Optional:

- Towels.
- Heat/ice packs.
- Pet first aid book.

This is merely a starting list for you. Think about what your dog needs medically day to day and in an emergency. Check with your vet as to what they would recommend including, and consider your local area and your dog's lifestyle for any extras—such as doggie sunscreen or tick removal devices.

Package all the items into the container and don't forget to label the kit with your vet's emergency contact number. Should you have an emergency on your hands, this saves precious time by allowing you to call the vet for help while attending to your dog.

Don't forget . . .

To clean out and review your first aid kit and any pet medications on a regular basis. Throughout the year it's easy to build up old tablets, powders, lotions, and potions for the family, and your pooch is no exception. Trouble is these medications go out of date (hello random bottle from 2005!), and using them when they have expired can be ineffective and downright dangerous for your dog.

So go through your home medical collection and dispose carefully of anything damaged or out of date. Not too sure about something? Contact your vet or err on the side of caution and safely get rid of it. Once the clean out is complete, now's the ideal time to stock up on treatments such as worming tablets or flea treatments for your at home kit, to ensure you have your dog's healthiest paw forward.

DOG FIRST AID COURSES. THEY'RE TOTALLY A THING.

From doggie CPR, to how to deal with broken limbs, choking, burns, and heat stroke, these courses can literally let you go all Meredith Grey on your dog in an emergency. Check with your vet for local classes and learn how to save a life.

Holistic Remedies

with Sarah Dickerson

Sarah Dickerson is a designer and creative director by trade, and a faith-filled, animal-loving, plant-based health enthusiast at heart. Her passion is to encourage others and to create things that bring joy and light. Sarah lives in Ohio with her husband Tanner and sweet Shih Tzu, Coco Bean.

How can Dog Mamas make their pet's environment less toxic?

Knowledge is power. Reading and researching ingredients and becoming aware of what you are using daily is a crucial starting point on the mission of reducing toxins in your and your dog's environment.

From the fabrics that we lay on, to household cleaners, food, detergents, shampoos, and everything in between, there are a lot of sneaky chemicals that we interact with every day. Now I am not saying you need to swap everything to toxin-free overnight. Baby steps are okay! Start small, go from there, and keep a positive attitude. Even the smallest change can make a huge impact!

What are your go-to holistic products for dogs?
Coco Bean's food consists of a dehydrated mixture of human-grade ingredients like wild-caught whitefish, fruit, and veggies. This results in a green beard after every meal but is totally worth it. Below are some of the additional things I add in daily for extra health benefits!

Turmeric
I love to add raw turmeric powder to Coco's food mixture daily to help reduce any pain and inflammation throughout her body. Reducing inflammation is so important for dogs in all stages of life since it can potentially lead to numerous chronic health issues. The earlier you can start reducing inflammation the better. Prevention is always key! Turmeric also enhances the body's natural antioxidants and promotes liver (detoxification), musculoskeletal, GI, and cardiovascular function. There is a reason this healing plant has been used for thousands of years. So many benefits! It definitely has earned its "superfood" status. I

buy turmeric in capsule form and add the powder to her food every morning. She doesn't even notice!

I recommend consulting with your dog's health care professional for their specific dosage.

Sea Vegetables

"Eat your (sea) greens"—it's good advice for all of us, including our dogs! Sea vegetables like spirulina and kelp are rich in vitamins, minerals, amino acids, and phytonutrients. Kelp lends a hand in balancing glandular function, boosting metabolism, aiding the body in tissue repair, and so much more. Consuming kelp consistently for more than three weeks can even potentially reduce the manifestation of fleas (what?!). Spirulina is a game changer for senior dogs, as it helps boost their immune system, reduce inflammation, and promote eye health. I add these in a raw powder form to Coco's food mixture every morning.

I recommend consulting with your dog's health care professional for their specific dosage.

Filtered Water

It sounds so simple, right? This daily necessity plays a big role in how our dog's body functions. They not only need water, but they need *good* water. The kind without the junk. Tap water can have numerous unwanted and health-hindering things lurking in it. Investing in a high-quality water filter is essential!

What healthy rituals does Coco have?

Monthly

She gets chiropractic adjustments! She (and I) are very fortunate that her dad is a chiropractor and can keep all of our nervous systems functioning optimally.

While I may not create beautiful "Instagram-worthy" food bowls on the daily, I do make sure that all of these additional ingredients get mixed into her food. Because nobody has time to make that every day! Once stirred up, it looks like a green mess in a bowl, but all she cares about is the taste. Thank goodness!

I would highly recommend researching in your area for a chiropractor who is trained to adjust pets!

Seasonally

During flea season I love diluting a little lemongrass oil with water and dabbing some on her collar and back. Sometimes I will even mist it on her dog bed and blanket as an extra step. It does a great job of warding off fleas, and the smell is mild enough not to bother her.

If dog mamas could do ONE thing to boost their dog's health and well-being, what would it be?

Consult with a holistic veterinarian who specializes in food therapy as well as herbal medicine to find out what types of whole foods are the right (and wrong) fit for your dog's biochemistry. We all have different biochemical makeups, and so do our dogs!

After we had Coco examined around the age of three, we found out that poultry, grains, and white potatoes had negative effects on her body. We switched her to fish and a grain-free, organic mixture of other whole foods and quickly saw such a vast improvement in her overall health, energy, and mood. She is now in her golden years and is still thriving. I cannot recommend this enough!

What one item could you, as a dog mama, not live without?

Lint rollers! Coco doesn't shed, however, she is a magnet for getting lint, dust, and dirt on her paws, and her paws are on my lap 99.99 percent of the time (but I wouldn't have it any other way).

Dog Photography

Camera Basics

Me buying a new phone . . .
Assistant: Do you want the 32GB or the 128GB?
Me: What's that in dog photos?

If modern technology tells us anything, a photographer with a good eye can use a phone camera to get an amazing shot.

Yet if you'd like to get started taking quality photos of your dog at home beyond your phone's capabilities (or your phone has literally run out of space), here's what you need to get started:

- A DSLR camera (most professionals use Canon or Nikon) with a midrage lens. Don't feel you have to buy an expensive camera or fancy lens to get started.
- Camera and lens-cleaning supplies. Because dogs are messy and you never know when a stray bit of fur or drool is going to hit.
- A backup drive/cloud storage. The last thing you want is to lose all your photos if your computer crashes!

Optional*:
- A macro lens—great for close ups of paws, eyes, noses, etc.
- Tripod—for static shots.
- Light reflector for eliminating shadows.

---

* As in may get left in the cupboard gathering dust along with your cake-making tools, cross fit gear, and whatever other hobbies that got abandoned after the initial excitement . . .

While it can be exciting to focus on fancy camera gear, the two things that will make or break your photos are lighting and composition.

Natural light will always be your best friend when taking photos of your dog. If indoors, opt for spaces in front of large windows where there is a good amount of natural light available. When outdoors, aim for the start or end of the day—either just before sunset or just after sunrise.

Pro Tip!

Professional dog photographers often opt for shooting in the afternoon, that gives them enough time to warm the dog up to the camera before the "golden hour" just before sunset arrives.

Good composition is your next step in achieving the perfect photo. To get an idea of composition start to look at your favorite dog photos—where is your eye drawn? What grabs your attention? You'll soon notice that most great photos incorporate these composition elements:

The rule of thirds. This involves imagining your image is cross-sectioned into nine equal parts. A good photo makes sure the point of interest of the photo (i.e., your pupper's face!) is placed where these lines intersect. As humans we don't naturally look to the center of a shot—using the rule of thirds works with our natural way of viewing an image for where the point of focus should be.

Balance. A well-composed image is all about balancing the main subject of your image (such as your dog) with the other elements. Placing your dog off center in the shot is often a good start to achieving this. From here take as many photos as you can from all sorts of angles. Get down on the floor, stand on a chair, exhaust every option you can think of. You'll soon start to see what shots work best for you and the look you're aiming for. The more shots you take, the more options you'll have—so have some fun!

What the heck is . . .

Warning! The next few paragraphs are all very technical sounding, and frankly all this jargon makes most people want to never take a photo again. But stay with me! It'll be over before you know it . . . and it *will* help you take better photos.

Aperture

To put it simply, aperture is the hole inside your camera lens that allows light to travel into the camera body. It works similarly to your own eye pupil. The larger the aperture, the more light passes through.

On your camera display, aperture is measured in "F-stops"–for example, f/2 or f/22.

How does aperture affect your doggo photos? Apertures that have a wider opening (more light) have a smaller F-Stop number (i.e., f/2) and are great for close-ups. So if you're wanting beautiful portrait shots of your pup that's the way to go. Whereas apertures with a smaller opening (less light) and a larger number (i.e., f/16) allows for much more of the image to be in focus–for example, a shot of your dog running in a field with a beautiful landscape behind them.

Shutter Speed

Shutter speed is the length of time a camera shutter is open to allow light to pass through and be captured by the camera sensor.

Faster shutter speeds generally work better for action shots of dogs running, playing, and generally being, you know, dogs. Experiment with your shutter speeds to see what you can capture without turning the whole image into one furry blur!

ISO

A strange little acronym, ISO basically means how sensitive your camera is to the current light source. For regular photos of your pup in natural daylight, aim for a low ISO. This avoids any graininess that comes with higher-ISO images and results in a clear, crisp image.

DITCH THE AUTO-MODE SHAME

Repeat after me. There is absolutely nothing wrong with shooting in auto mode. Especially when we're talking about photographing pets.

Yes, learning about aperture, shutters speeds, ISO—and all the elements of shooting in manual mode—is worthwhile. But when you're starting out, using auto mode allows you to focus on your subject and the shot you want, without getting overwhelmed by all the buttons and dials.

Pet photography is not the same as food, or portrait photography. You're dealing with squiggly, moving, distracted dogs and when the right shot comes up you need to be ready. Auto mode allows you to do that.

Once you start to feel comfortable with capturing the compositions you desire, only then begin experimenting with other modes to experience their benefits.

Cameras have come a long way in recent decades, and even professional photographers will now admit that you can get beautiful, well-composed photos while shooting on auto.

So ditch the shame! Switch to auto proudly and get the photo you want.

Pro Tips for a No-Tears Photo Shoot . .

- Always have treats and toys on hand to keep your pooch interested.
- Take your photos in short bursts so your pet doesn't get bored.
- Make the experience fun for your dog. Never put them in situations where they are uncomfortable—they won't be happy, and it will show in the photo.
- Reward your pet with a walk or game following the photo shoot. This will lead them to associating photos with fun!
- Take lots of photos from all different angles. Just think—if you take twenty photos, at least one has to be good!
- Relax and enjoy the process. Remember, you're capturing memories, but you're also creating them.

How to Get Your Dog to Look at the Camera

If you've ever tried to take a cute photo of your dog only to have them look at the floor (yep), that shifty bird in the tree behind you (double yep), or basically anything other than the camera you're pointing at them, these expert tips are for you.

Photos where our dogs are looking straight down the lens have the power to connect, showing their true personality.

After decades of watching professional pet photographers do their thing, I've learned a trick or two totally transferrable to us regular folk at home who *just-want-one-nice-photo-of-the-dog-thank-you-very-much.*

1. Treat Yo' Dog

Just like nearly everything else related to dogs, treats are a go-to number one option when trying to encourage your dog to do something new. It's like dogs like food or something.

To use your treats, set up the photo you want to take and show your dog the treats you have in your hand. Get your pup to sit, drop, or however you want them to pose, then slowly step back holding your treat just above the camera lens with your other hand. You dog will naturally not take their eyes away from the treat, leaving you to snap away.

2. Make Some Noise

The best thing about this way of getting your dog's attention? You don't need anything else—just you.

When you're ready to take your photo, start making a variety of noises every few seconds. These noises can be anything from clicking your tongue, to trilling like a bird, or barking like a dog. Your dog, thinking you're going slightly mad, will immediately look at you. Try all sorts of noises until you find what works

best for you. Experiment as much as possible with all sorts of sounds. Yes, you'll sound and look crazy, but you'll soon find out what noises work to get eye contact, head tilts, lifted ears, and all kinds of doggo reactions that make for gorgeous photos.

Attention words, such as "dinner," "walk," and "treat," also have the same effect here,

however sometimes can result in an annoyed dog realizing they're being played when no dinner, walks, or treats are actually forthcoming. Best to use sparingly. Nothing's worse than a temperamental star.

Same goes for actually calling your dog's name. For some dogs this works a treat, however for others they will immediately get up and walk over to you. Play around and work out what words, noises, and phrases work best for you and your pup.

If you're planning on taking your dog's photo a lot and have aspirations of them being the Cindy Crawford of the dog modeling world, consider training them to look at the camera on demand. Simply say a command word, such as "look," and when your dog looks at the camera, reward them with a treat. Practice this, and over time they will soon learn the command word requires them to look at the camera . . . and you have yourself a doggie supermodel!

3. Squeakers, Toys, and Whistles

To up the ante, many professional photographers turn to props to get that pupper eye contact.

You can start with your dog's favorite toy (or a totally new toy!) and hold it just above the camera lens. This works especially well for visually motivated pups such as herding dogs who will lock eyes on their favourite ball and nothing will make them turn away.

Toys with squeakers, rattles, and other sounds work effectively here too. You're basically outsourcing those weird noises you were making earlier, now with a visual distraction as well.

Lastly, a variety of whistles and noisemakers will guarantee a doggo's attention. I've seen photographers who wear lanyards filled with a variety of whistles and kazoos that make every kind of sound known to man. From ducks sounds to high-pitched whistles, they slowly run through the sounds to see what the dog responds to and then grab their perfect shot.

4. Try Your Phone

Not every photo needs to be a professional shoot with a handheld camera. In fact with the quality of phone cameras and software these days, phone photos can be amazing. And, it can be much easier to capture a cute snap of your dog on the fly with your phone, without the cumbersome setup of a digital camera. For those with an iPhone, portrait mode even enables you to capture your pup with a nice blurry (bokeh) background in one tap.

There are a number of products on the market these days that can attach to your phone to keep your dog's attention. These "pet selfie stick" attachments hold balls, treats, and toys to encourage your dog to look at the lens.

Additionally, there are several free noisemaker apps that you can download on your phone and use in place of vocal noises and real-life whistles.

5. Practice Makes Perfect

The biggest tip any photographer will tell you is, the more time your dog spends around cameras, the more comfortable they will be. Short, fun photo sessions are the key here. When your dog is comfortable and relaxed they will respond better to sounds, treats, and toys. If you find yourself getting frustrated, just try again another time. Your dog can pick up on anxiety, and no one wants to hang a sad dog photo on the wall.

Always be flexible in the shot you are trying to get. Sometimes the best photos are the ones where the dog does something totally unexpected! Having patience in the process allows you to be ready to capture that one-in-a-million photo when it happens.

Handy Hint

If you're finding it all too much to hold treats, toys, whistle, *and* focus the camera, consider roping in a helper. Your photography assistant can stand or crouch beside you holding the treats or toys above the lens while you just concentrate on getting the perfect shot. Plus it gives you someone to yell at when things go wrong (it's a dream job for them, I know).

At-Home Photography

While nothing beats a professional pet photography session to have keepsake photos that you will always treasure, there's something special about photos that you're able to capture yourself at home.

With your dog completely relaxed, their favorite person (you!) by their side, you're in the prime position to capture all those distinctive details only you know about. These photos allow your dog to show off their quirks and everyday habits and allows you to capture a true reflection of their personality you only see at home.

But there's no mistaking it, home pet photography can be hard. You need to work with the space, light, and decor you have. And unless you have a long-suffering Instagram husband, there's no assistant helping you set up the perfect shot.

Style Your Space

Take a look at many of your favorite doggo accounts on social media and you'll see that very few live in lavish mansions in which to take beautiful photos of their pet.

In fact, look closely and you'll see many of them have just a few spots in their homes where they have good light to take photos.

What do they do that's different? They bring out their inner stylist.

You don't need to create a doggie studio, but by styling the space in which you take photos of your dog at home, you create a cohesive aesthetic that makes your at-home photos unique to you.

Some ideas include:

- Styling your bed or sofa with lots cushions and throws to give a colorful backdrop to your dog. This is especially great for capturing sleepy, snuggly shots.
- Getting fresh flowers from the market and including them in your photo frame to add a pop of color.
- Using different floor rugs to add texture and color to your photos.
- Buy a meter or two of your favorite fabric and choose a softly lit area of your home to set up. Hang or tape the fabric to the wall, letting it fall to the ground. Pop your dog in front and start snapping!

All of these can be switched up on demand, meaning you never run out of fresh looks.

Look for Details

The one thing you'll always be better at than any professional pet photographer is knowing your dog.

You know their right ear flips up higher than the left one. You know how cute they look when they're sleeping. You know they once stole your roommate's underwear off the washing line and neither of you told anyone. You know everything inside and out. These little details are the ones you'll forever hold in your heart, so it's time to capture them on film.

Take advantage of the fact that your dog will allow you to get closer to them than anyone else with a camera. Experiment with close-up shots of their eyes, nose, ears, and paws. Capture that head tilt they do when you say the word "walk." Use your camera to try different angles and degrees of focus. Take lots of photos and start to get a feel for the ones that resonate.

You'll soon find these shots capture your dog's essence more than any other image.

Use Props

When wolves first starting living alongside humans all those years ago, they probably never imagined their descendants would end up spending their days posing for photos wearing crazy hats and matching sweaters. But here we are.

The good thing to know, you can have fun with props without heading over into total crazy dog lady territory (*not that there's anything wrong with that*).

These days, there are so many fun dog toys that pull double duty as photo props, your job is half done. From plush bottles of rosé, to stuffed donuts, you can create a fun story within a photo using your dog's favorite toys.

Another great option is the mini chalkboard. Personalized and hung around your dog's neck, it's a great way to share a message, such as an engagement, new baby, or graduation from puppy preschool.

From here you can be as creative as you want—hats, glasses, collars, bandanas, bow ties, flower crowns—there are a myriad of prop options to make your at-home photography a bit more fun. (See page 113 for my DIY dog collar sleeves).

Capture Your Day

Some of the loveliest photo memories you'll have are the everyday moments snapped on the go. Use your phone, or leave your camera out for easy access to capture your dog sneaking a nap on the couch. Or snuggling with their favorite human. Or barking at the squirrels in the neighbor's tree.

These are the moments that make up your authentic lives together. You'll treasure them forever.

Edit Your Pics

Even the best photographers with the fanciest equipment edit their photos. While you don't have to edit each and every photo you take, consider it for your favorites—the ones you'll hang on your walls, share with friends, or put in albums.

These days it's never been easier to edit at-home photos. There are a number of free apps for phone photos (my favorites include Lightroom and VSCO) and desktop versions of Lightroom and Photoshop can be purchased on a subscription basis. While they may look intimidating, a few online tutorials will teach you all you need to know about brightening, sharpening, and boosting the color and vibrancy of your images.

Be warned though—once you start editing your photos, you'll love the difference so much, you'll never turn back!

WHAT'S A FLAT LAY?

A stalwart of the magazine era, and now made insanely popular by Instagram, flat-lay photos are images taken from above featuring items laid flat on a surface. A great way to include your dog in a flat-lay is to have their paws in frame laying flat on the same surface. Alternatively, you can arrange favorite items around a very still or sleeping dog for a fun effect!

DIY: Doggy Photo Accessories

Collar sleeves are a simple way to update your dog's look for fun photos. Making your own allows you to choose the fabrics and trims that best suit your pup—and they're budget-friendly. These no-sew collar sleeves are easy to make, and designed to slip on and off your favorite collars so your pup is sure to always be in style.

No-Sew Collar Sleeves

You'll Need:

- Fabric scraps
- Your choice of ribbon, trim, or sequins
- Scissors
- Hot glue & glue gun
- Dog collar

Method:

1. Gather fabric scraps or remnants from your local fabric store. Use your dog's collar to measure how much fabric you will need to wrap around it. If your collar has a buckle, be sure you leave enough room so that you don't cover the buckle holes.
2. Wrap your fabric around the collar so that the ends overlap one another—this part is very important, you don't want to get any hot glue on your collar! Trim excess fabric. Place a thin line of hot glue between the two overlapping layers and press down gently to bond. Once your sleeve is glued it should look just like a sleeve/tube, and it should easily slide on and off of your collar.
3. Next is the fun part! If you want to add a bit of glam to your sleeve, try adding your choice of ribbon or trim. Secure with a bit of hot glue and let set to dry.

@honeyidressedthepug
www.honeyidressedthepug.com
www.ariandm.com

Pet Fashion
with Maitri Mody

With her pug, Ari, Maitri Mody is the creator of the enormously successful Instagram account Honey I Dressed the Pug—their dog mom & pup twinning looks earning them devoted fans across the globe. With a bachelor's degree in international trade & marketing for fashion industries from the Fashion Institute of Technology (FIT), Maitri has worked in the fashion industry for more than fifteen years as designer, fashion stylist, and in wholesale production. Following their Insta-stardom, Maitri launched her own pet accessories brand—Ari & M, which offers stylish contemporary accessories for both human & dogs. Originally from Mumbai, India, Maitri now lives in New York City with her husband and Ari.

What are your top tips for making pet fashion fun?

Invest in good pet brands that use high-quality material so that your pet does not get harmed due to harsh dyes, fabrics that are not breathable, etc.

Along with clothes, invest in some good accessories, so when it's too hot to wear clothes, your pet can still look stylish.

Always make sure your dog is comfortable in clothes because not all dogs like to dress up.

Nowadays more and more kids are wearing mini versions of adult fashion rather than out-n-out kids' clothes, which looks super cool. So instead of making your dog wear clothes that look childish, go for more chic and grown-up styles.

Match your clothes with your dog in some way either by color coordinating or wearing similar prints. If you prefer being more subtle, then match accessories like your shoes with their bow tie. It's super fun!

What does every dog need in his or her wardrobe?

Denim accessories (collar + leash + bandana, since they go with everything), rain jacket or winter coat or both (based on where you live), striped tee, bright sweater, and a chic bow tie.

What are your favorite organization & storage hacks for dog clothes and accessories?

I bought a $15 clothing rack from Ikea and some small size baby hangers and it works well to hang Ari's day-to-day wardrobe. I fold other clothes and accessories and store them in clear plastic boxes. I am always looking for new solutions to fit Ari's ever-expanding wardrobe. I think he has more clothes than me!

What do you look for in quality pet apparel and accessories?

Fit and finish are the most important aspects for me. The way a garment fits can easily separate the good brands from low-quality brands.

The finish and quality should be at par with human clothing or even better since there is more wear and tear.

Dogs are pretty much like kids—they like to run, roll in the grass, get into mud . . . the clothes need to hold up.

Any pet fashion "Don'ts"?

Don't make them wear clothes that are too tight or restrict movement; always leave at least a couple of inches breathing room.

When It's Time to Call in the Professionals . . .

How to Choose a Pet Photographer.

While at-home photos are amazing, there is something special about a professional pet photography session. Pro dog photographers have access to an arsenal of photographic knowledge, composition, and editing us mere mortals just don't have.

But pro photographers do come in a variety of styles and standards. Here's how to get more of "OMG I want to blow up that photo of Millie the Doxie and put it on my wall" and less of "these photos are going to end up on awkwarddogphotos.com."

Think About the Why

When choosing a pet photographer, the first thing you need to decide is why you are getting professional photos of your pup. Is it to capture them as a puppy? Is it to get quality photos to display in your home? Is it for keepsake imagery of a beloved senior dog? Having a clear focus of what kind of photos you'd like gives you an easy reference point to go back to as you begin your search.

Choose Your Style

There are so many pet photography styles that there is no one-size-fits-all option. Think about the photo styles you like in magazines, or admire in other people's homes.

Do you like light-filled, bright photography? Or sepia-toned images? Or dramatic black-and-white photos? Do you like detailed artistic shots, or happy family snaps? Do you want photos of you snuggling at home, or a stylized studio shoot?

Start a vision board with the kind of shots you'd like, and once you start to see a theme developing, start looking for local photographers who shoot in this style. Googling and scouring social media is a place to start, but don't forget to ask for recommendations from friends, your groomer, and other dog owners you meet at the park.

Do Your Research

Once you find a photographer you like, look further into their online presence. Do they have favorable reviews? Have they come recommended from a trusted source? Are they set up as a professional business? Do they respond politely and in a timely manner? Do they have a studio where you can see their finished work on display?

Comparing packages and price is a good starting point, but making sure you're going to be happy with the final result is the ultimate goal.

Always be guided by your gut feeling on a photographer. You want this person to be professional, courteous and to "click" with both yourself and your dog. There is nothing worse than having your photo taken by a person you don't feel comfortable with.

Do What's Best for Your Dog

Before locking in a photographer, take a beat to think about your dog's point of view.

You may love the idea of a dramatic photoshoot of your dog out and about in nature, but if your dog gets anxious in unfamiliar places, a photographer who can come to your home is probably a better option.

A comfortable dog is a happy dog. And a happy dog takes the best photos.

Look at the Fine Print

Do you really need that USB stick of every photo from the session? What quality paper does the photographer print on? Can they use your image in their marketing or social media pages?

Always double-check the fine print to know what exactly you are getting and the photographer's obligations to you once the shoot is done.

THE ONE THING EVERYONE FORGETS . . .

We get so focused on finding the perfect photographer to take photos of our dog, that we forget to ask if we'll be in the photo. Some photographers who are amazing at dog shots, can be pretty average at taking human photos. It's just not their specialty (and you know your dog is totes going to tag you in the pic where they look good and you look like a troll that lives under a bridge). If you want your photo session to include images of you *and* your dog, always make sure you choose a photographer who has extensive experience in both people and pet photography.

Prep Like a Pro—Getting Ready for a Professional Photoshoot

Feeling cute, might get a professional photo shoot and destroy some shoes later, idk.

Have a Game Plan

Before you even book your photographer, know what photos you want to get out of the session. Is it for your annual holiday card? An updated session for the family gallery wall? Knowing how you plan to use the photos will make it easier to communicate to your photographer what you need.

If you're after a specific setup or composition of photo, it's always a good idea to show your photographer an example ahead of time so they can let you know if it is achievable or not.

Pre-Shoot Prep

Book your dog in for a groom (or do it at home) a few days before the shoot. Advise your groomer you want a neat, presentable look for photos—don't let them go overboard with clipping. A neat trim? Yes. An overzealous haircut that has no time to grow out before the shoot? Nope.

On the day, take time to brush your dog, wipe away any unsightly eye discharge or drool. Take your brush and wipes with you for any last-minute touch-ups.

Don't forget to take some time out to focus on grooming yourself! Even if you weren't intending on being in the photos, chances are you might be in some. Make your hair, makeup, and outfit (including your shoes, which easily get in lots of shots by default!) presentable. If your shoot is themed (i.e., it's going to be your Christmas card) make sure any outfits and accessories planned for you and your dog are cohesive and work together as a whole.

On the Day

To burn off any nervous energy, take your dog on a good walk before the photo session—this goes double for high-energy doggos. A calm, relaxed dog will allow the photographer to get better "in focus" images and will make it easier for your dog to listen and follow commands.

Things to Bring

Number one on your list? Be sure to bring your dog's absolute favorite treats. Not the everyday treats—the high-reward yummy treats (like cooked chicken) they only get on special occasions. These treats will encourage your pupper to follow instructions and help your photographer get the best out of them.

If your shoot is themed (i.e., birthday, holiday card, etc.) talk with your photographer about bringing props—this could be anything from your dog's favorite toy to a holiday sweater. Your photographer will often have great suggestions and ideas of what works in this department so chat to them prior about it.

Basic essentials such as a water bowl, brush, wipes, collar, and leash round out your list.

Don't Forget

To let your photographer know ahead of time if your dog has special needs. Does your dog get nervous around other dogs? Do they love the beach or hate the sight of water? Are they easily distracted and need a secluded location? Do they come back when called or must stay on the leash? (Remember, leashes can be photo-shopped out!)

The more information you can provide your photographer, the more planning they can put into making sure the shoot location and photography is suitable for your pup.

And once that camera starts clicking? Relax. If you relax, it will be easier for your dog to as well! Have fun, enjoy the moment, and follow your photographer's lead. Oh, and don't forget to smile.

Photographing Puppies

I can't think of any dog mama in history who has looked back and said, "I wish I didn't take that many puppy photos." The puppy stage is one that is so fleeting—it's over before you know it (yes, this sounds like a lie when you're toilet training a puppy . . .). So there's never a better time to capture that sweet, sweet pupper goodness in photo form.

But it's not easy. They are literally wriggling balls of fluff that take absolutely zero direction. Herding cats is easier. But with these tips, you can make it happen.

1. Tire Out Your Puppy

A wise dog mama once said, "Puppies have two settings: full throttle and off." Truer words have never been spoken. It's almost impossible to get a puppy to sit still or follow commands; you just have to go with the flow (I have half a memory card of blurry puppy photos to prove this).

To get a chance of having even half of your puppy photos in focus, be sure to follow puppies closely and be ready to snap that picture when they start to get tired.

Snuggle them, play with them, tire them out, and when they start to get sleepy, pick up your camera. What a terrible way to spend an afternoon.

2. Props are Your Friend

Professionals swear by props—baskets, crates, and small benches—to keep puppies contained in one area. A contained puppy is much easier to photograph than a puppy roaming freely.

As an added bonus, puppies in basket? Cuteness guaranteed.

3. Capture their Attention

Give puppies something to focus on and you'll not only slow them down, but you'll capture that puppy-like wonderment only they have.

Puppies love to explore, and (ensuring they're tired enough from Tip #1) giving them a new toy to investigate or a pupcake to smell can make for some cute shots of these little critters discovering the big world around them. Extra cute points if the prop is bigger than the puppy.

Pro Tip!

Don't forget to get some shots of mama (or papa) dog if they are available.

Any doggo that brings multiple puppies into this world deserves some photo credit, and these family shots will be treasured keepsakes for years to come.

What Is an Angel Session?

An angel session is a professional pet photography shoot for your much-loved dog in their later years. For many dogs these pet portrait sessions follow a terminal diagnosis and can even be a last-minute photo shoot in their final days.

It's an incredibly sad thing to think about, yet angel sessions are a bittersweet opportunity to celebrate your furry soulmate and create photo memories that you can treasure forever.

For some dogs, it may be their first ever photoshoot. Life can get busy and a lot of dog owners don't always think to get professional photos of their pets.

While photos at any age are a beautiful keepsake, professional pet photographers agree that angel sessions are the most beloved of all their work.

If you have an elderly pup, consider getting an angel session. If you talk to dog owners who have farewelled fur-children, they'll tell you it's something they never regret.

To make this heartfelt moment easier, some thoughts to consider include:

- Find a photographer you love that does angel sessions now—prior to needing a booking. Pop their details away for later.
- If you don't do the above, don't feel like you can't contact a photographer at the last minute. Many professionals leave spaces in their calendar for these types of sessions and can often do the photo shoot with very little notice. They know how important it is to dog moms and dads.
- Be prepared to be in some of the photos. You are capturing the bond between you and your pet, after all. If you can be critical of your appearance in photos, make an effort with your styling on the day to feel good. Let the photographer know if you are self-conscious of anything in particular and they can frame the photo accordingly. Some of the most beautiful shots of senior dogs feature just a hand stroking their fur, or the back of a head during a cuddle. You don't want to miss out on a heartfelt photo with your beloved dog because you're worried about how you look.
- Choose a shooting location that is familiar to your pup. You don't want to put any extra stress on them. Shooting at home often works the best, as you can capture your dog in their favorite nap spot, or with their most treasured toy. Your photographer can also photograph your dog's food bowls, leash, and collar to preserve their memory.
- While an angel session can come at a heartbreaking time, try to focus on the good times you've shared with your pet and the love you have for them. It will shine through in your photos.

@hellohoku
foxandbagel.com

Instagram Photography

with Jen Ha

Jen Ha is a freelance graphic designer, founder of design studio Fox & Bagel and dog mom to a spunky Shiba Inu named Hoku. They live in sunny Southern California and enjoy growing vegetables, hiking through the woods, and a solid avocado toast.

What are your favorite tips for creating a cohesive, beautiful, and unique Instagram feed?

A consistent aesthetic and an authentic voice goes a long way. I'd say that the most important thing is being true to your own unique perspective instead of solely following social media photography trends.

What tips do you have for dog owners new to Instagram wanting to create a beautiful and popular account for their dog?

I really believe people are drawn to originality and authenticity.

Don't start an account for the sole purpose of becoming popular and monetizing it, but do it because you love capturing and sharing the everyday moments with your pup with others. In the process, hone your aesthetic and find your voice (be it conversational, humorous, informative, or even silly "dog speak") and the right audience will find you.

As a pro photographer, what are your expert tips for capturing photos for Instagram?

I use my phone for Instagram Stories and my DSLR for my Instagram feed. My go-to apps for editing for Stories are Snapseed, A Color Story, and Unfold. With my feed, I edit primarily in Photoshop.

I love natural, diffused, even lighting so partly cloudy days are my jam. With dog photography, I use continuous high speed or burst mode to really make sure I'm able to capture the perfect moment.

With composition, one of my favorite things to do is frame a shot with foliage.

Don't be afraid to try different angles and perspectives to get the framing just right, even it means lying on the ground or really getting into the leaves.

Sure, some passersby may think you're a crazy person but as they say, "anything for the 'gram"–*within reason, of course!* Always be safe and respectful of others, of property, of the rules.

Your work is fun and creative while still being aesthetically beautiful. What work goes into a photo on your feed?

I love using what's available around me when it comes to props and knowing what time of day will produce the best light. I try to keep my images relevant to our daily lives and what we're loving at the moment so I don't usually find myself buying things solely for placing into an Instagram image.

When I find myself needing to shoot something for commercial purposes, however (for instance, a book that needs to stay open or a round object that needs to stay in place), I've found mounting putty to be incredibly useful.

What three things does every great dog Instagrammer need?

1. Camera (phone or DSLR) and editing apps.
2. Something your dog will look at–be it treats, toys, or something that makes a funny sound.
3. A clean background (a little bit of tidying before taking a photo goes a long way–be it taking a twig out of the frame or hiding a tissue box).

What one item could you, as a dog mama, not live without?

A good pair of walking shoes, because a tired pup is a happy pup!

Pet Travel

Choosing Pet-Friendly Vacation Stays

When surveyed, nine out of ten dogs agreed they'd stop chewing up their owners' things, if they were taken on more vacations.*

Still, there's never been a better time than now to get away with your dog in tow. With the boom of pet-friendly vacation rentals, you and your pup are literally spoiled for choice.

Beach destinations, city escapes, country retreats . . . you and your dog can have it all.

Start Your Search

The best way to start your pet-friendly vacation search is heading both online and offline. In real life ask friends, family, and (friendly, normal-looking) randoms at the dog park for their favorite pet-friendly vacation suggestions. Online, ask on social media and search the pet-friendly homes listed on Airbnb and other vacation rental sites.

Things to consider include:

- The location—do you want to be near dog-friendly parks or beaches?
- The size—do you want space for your pup to run free? Or would you prefer to know where they are at all times?

---

* No they didn't. In fact, they just chewed up the paper the survey was printed on.

- The layout—are there stairs, open balconies, or other elements that your dog may have trouble with?
- The furnishings—are they dog-friendly, or are you going to be stressed constantly that your pup is ruining the bespoke herringbone flooring?

While you're looking for an amazing vacation spot, remember your dog is going to be the same whether they're home or away. A fancy apartment may look like a dream destination, but if you're bringing a slobber machine that will ruin the plush carpet and knock over that priceless ornament in two seconds flat . . . maybe consider a property more suitable for you and your dog.

Pet-Friendly? For Real?

Found the perfect place? Now it's your job to check that it's really pet-friendly. Read up on any vacation rental forums and you'll discover not all of them are as pupper-friendly as they say.

Things to look for include:

- Are dogs allowed inside the property? (Yes, there are some people who rent out "pet-friendly" properties who don't allow this!)
- Will there be other pets living at the property during your stay? (Again, this actually happens.)
- If there are external areas, are they fully fenced and secured?
- Do these areas have adequate shade and protection from the elements?

- Is there a safe space for your dog to toilet?
- Can your dog be left unattended at the property?
- Do they provide bowls, beds, or other doggo amenities? Some properties even provide old towels for muddy paws!

Check out reviews for the property to see what prior guests with pets have said. Guest photos are often a great indication of the real vacation rental you are getting.

Always feel comfortable to ask the host any questions you may have when making the booking. Clearing up any questions or gray areas prior to your stay means you can relax and enjoy when you arrive!

Pro Tip!

When you arrive at your pet-friendly vacation stay, take a quick photo or video tour of the property to document the condition it is in. That way, any prior damage is noted and can't be blamed on your perfect pooch!

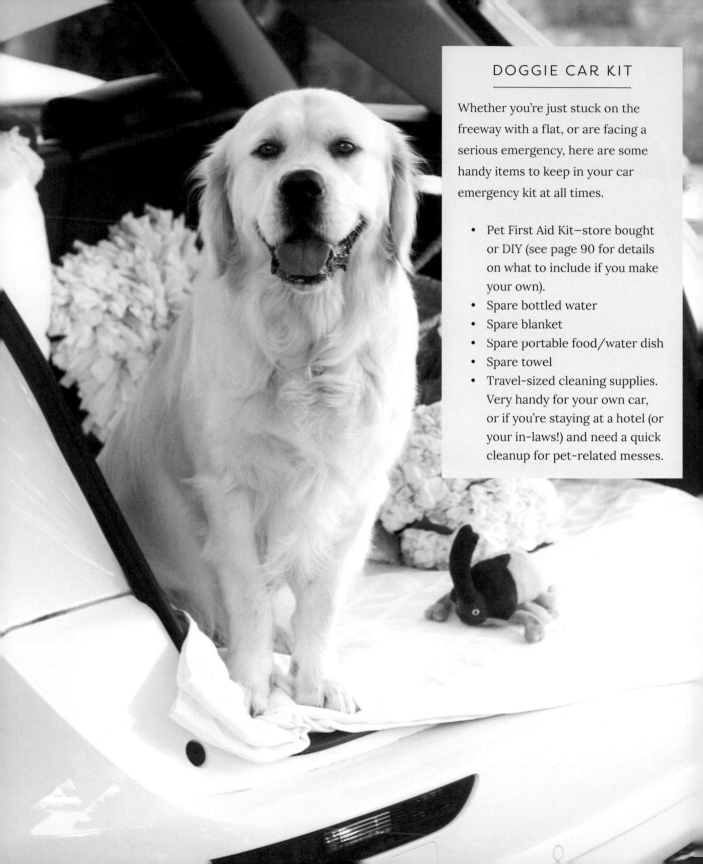

DOGGIE CAR KIT

Whether you're just stuck on the freeway with a flat, or are facing a serious emergency, here are some handy items to keep in your car emergency kit at all times.

- Pet First Aid Kit—store bought or DIY (see page 90 for details on what to include if you make your own).
- Spare bottled water
- Spare blanket
- Spare portable food/water dish
- Spare towel
- Travel-sized cleaning supplies. Very handy for your own car, or if you're staying at a hotel (or your in-laws!) and need a quick cleanup for pet-related messes.

Car Travel 101

They see me rollin', they hatin' . . .

Whether you're planning a Griswold-style road trip, or a quick weekender, having your dog comfortable and safe in the car is a must. But with a bit of planning and organization you'll be flying down that freeway with Fido in no time.

Before You Go

When planning your car trip, always keep your dog in mind:

- Double-check their microchip information and make sure their dog tags have the most up-to-date info for you.
- If your trip involves overnight travel, ensure any motels/accommodations you are planning to stay at are pet-friendly (and your dog is booked in!)
- Make a note of emergency vets along your travel route and ensure you have their contact details.
- Do some research on the places you are visiting to see if they have great dog-friendly areas—from off-leash parks, to dog-friendly cafés or beaches. That way if you have free time you can enjoy it with your pup.

Pimp Your Ride

While I'm sure your dog would appreciate a nice spoiler and custom rims on your car, I'm actually talking car safety. The number one thing you always need to do when transporting your dog is to secure them safely in the vehicle. It could be a five-minute trip to the vet or a five-day hiking vacation—either way your dog needs to be safe and comfortable. Your options include:

Car harness and seat belt attachment. Every dog traveling in a car needs to be restrained—gone are the days where your doggo could roam about the cabin. And while photos of puppies asleep on the console look adorable, they're actually a dangerous projectile waiting to happen. A soft chest plate harness is always preferable over a collar as it puts less strain on the neck and joints in the case of sudden jolts and crashes. Always ensure your harness is the correct size and properly fitted. It needs to allow your pet to sit and lie down comfortably while still keeping them restrained in case of an accident.

Booster seat. These little gems create a safe space for smaller dogs within the back seat of your car. Similar to children's booster seats, these car seats allow your dog to sit up higher and look out the window while being safely restrained.

Car seat hammock. For larger dogs, hammocks are a great option. They hang between the back of the front seat and the front of the back seat—you simply slide them over the headrests and voila, car hammock! With zippered sides and velcro openings for the seat belt attachment, hammocks keep your dog from falling in the foot well and trying to jump into the front, while still allowing you easy access and interaction. Opt for waterproof versions to protect your upholstery.

Soft carriers, travel crates, and boot cages. All of these options involve keeping your pupper fully contained. For dogs that enjoy the safety of a crate or carrier, they can be an ideal option. When choosing your carrier or crate, always ensure it has proper ventilation and a leak-proof base. Make sure it is large enough for your dog to stand and move around in, and can be safely anchored to your car. Lastly, always pad them out with soft beds and blankets to keep your pup comfy! (See page 143 on how to introduce your dog to a carrier.)

Pro Tip!

Never allow your dog to travel in the front seat of your car if it is fitted with airbags. This could be fatal for your pet in an accident.

What to Pack

Whether your drive is a trip to the beach, or a cross-country expedition, these basics will get you started. Then you can simply add any extra elements your dog may need for your specific trip:

- Portable travel bowls for food and water—opt for collapsible bowls to save room.
- Dog food and water—I like to carry ours in the all-in-one Snack Duo Bottle for small day trips. One half keeps treats and/or dry food, while the other holds fresh water. With a handy pop up bowl clipped on, your dog always has somewhere to eat and drink with no spills or fuss. If your trip requires you to bring larger quantities of food, use an airtight container or Ziploc bag and opt for dry or dehydrated food. Always have extra water bottles on hand for emergencies.
- Treats
- Leash
- Spare collar with extra ID tag
- Favorite toy/s
- Soft bed and blanket
- Microfiber towel (super absorbent and quick drying) and wet wipes
- Waste bags
- Car emergency kit/first aid kit
- Any medications your dog may be on—with enough for the full trip plus extra.
- Copies of vaccination and ID papers—I used to think having this kind of information was excessive, however if your dog has an accident or you are traveling across borders, boy do they come in handy! Pop them on your phone or a USB if it's easier.

DOG MEETS CAR

Getting your dog used to the car is one of the most valuable lessons they can learn. While it's ideally done as a puppy, even old dogs can totally learn new tricks.

Start by allowing your dog to sit in the stationary car with you by their side. Introduce them to the car harness, hammock, or restraint you plan to use. Reward any calm behavior with treats and positive reinforcement. Lots of "good boys" will work a treat here!

Once they are comfortable in the space, start with a quick trip around the block. Next time try a five-minute trip that ends at a fun destination–like their favorite park or a Beyoncé concert. Slowly introduce longer car rides over a period of time until they are at ease with the journey.

If your dog shows any signs of motion sickness (vomiting, excessive drooling) chat with your vet about the best options for future trips.

Remember, some dogs will love car trips, others will be nervous, and some doggos may downright hate it. But the fact of life is, they're going to need to hop in the car every once in a while. Work with your dog's individual preferences to make it the best experience possible for everyone.

Hit the Road!

Keeping your doggo happy when you're on the road keeps everyone happy. Some tips you'll all enjoy the benefits of include:

Giving your dog a new interactive toy on day one of the road trip can keep them stimulated and occupied, while bringing an old toy provides comfort and eases stress.

Schedule extra rest stops for your dog to relieve themselves, grab a drink, and stretch their legs. If you can, try to add a short walk during one stop.

Never leave your dog alone in the car (they *will* change your radio station on you).*

---

* *But seriously. Never leave your dog alone in a car. Dogs can and have died in cars left unattended. Don't do it.*

How to Introduce Your Dog to a Carrier

For dogs and carriers, you're going to fall into one of two categories. Either your dog will hop in the carrier first go and totally love it, or . . . your dog will see the carrier as the scariest thing they have ever met and want you to rid this evil from their life immediately.

Experts all agree—if you're facing option one, have a cocktail and enjoy a lie down. But if you happen to fall into category two, here's your game plan . . .

Step One: The Carrier Is Totally Fine

Leaving the carrier out in the open in a high-traffic area for your dog (such as the living room or bedroom) for a few days will allow your dog to walk up to it, inspect it, and sniff it at their own pace, most likely when you aren't hovering. They'll soon start to realize that the earth won't fall to pieces over this strange new object.

Step Two: The Carrier Is Totally Fun

Once your dog can tolerate being close to the carrier without dashing for the nearest exit, it is time to up the ante. Start by placing treats and toys near the carrier and work up to placing them inside the carrier for your dog to enjoy. Always allow your dog full control at this stage, and don't attempt to zip them up or restrain them in the carrier just yet.

Reward them with positive praise when they are calm and happy around the carrier, and keep the treats coming!

Step Three: The Carrier Comes with Me

When your pup has reached the understanding that the carrier is a safe object with only positive connotations, try placing it in the car while it's stationary. Pop it where they normally sit so they can go in and out of it as they please. They will start to understand that this is an item that travels with them and it won't come as a shock when it shows up on your next trip.

Step Four: The Carrier is My Safe Place

Once your dog is voluntarily going inside their carrier and appears comfortable, try closing it halfway and reward them with a treat. If they are still cool, close it all the way for a few seconds and then open it back up. Lots of treats and positive praise here will work wonders.

Keep repeating this on a daily basis until they are BFFs with the carrier. Let them go back and forth and never force them. Before long, they will come to see the carrier as their own personal doggy den. Once they have had time to bond with it, your dog will view their carrier as a safe space to enjoy for many trips to come.

MY DOG IS HOME ALONE

If I am sick or injured in an Emergency Situation, please contact the individual listed on the back of this card to care for my dog at home.

DIY: My Dog Is Home Alone Card

Whether you're just going to work, or headed out on the vacation of a lifetime, these little cards could just be the thing that saves your dog's life. If something happens to you and you don't come home as expected, who knows to look out for your favorite furry friend?

With one small piece of paper, you, dog mama, get peace of mind that should the worst happen, emergency personnel will have the info they need to make sure your pooch is cared for. Simply print it out and pop it in your purse or wallet to know your dog will never be forgotten in an emergency.

Details to Include:

FRONT:

My Dog is Home Alone
If I am sick or injured in an emergency situation, please contact the individual listed on the back of this card to care for my dog at home.

BACK:
Name and number of at least one, preferably two, emergency contacts.

Don't Forget!
Confirm with your emergency contacts listed on the back of the card so they know to expect such a call should anything ever happen to you. Consider if they would need keys and/or access to your property if they were called on to help care for your dog at home.

If you're going on vacation, remind your emergency contacts and provide a copy of your itinerary and pet care details in your absence. That way your emergency contact can liaise with your hotel, pet-friendly rental, or pet sitter if required to ensure your dog gets looked after no matter what.

Free Printable
To download and print your very own card like the one pictured, head to prettyfluffy.com and search for "My Dog Is Home Alone Card."

Jet-Setting Pet Tips

Want to know how the people like Kendall Jenner look so effortlessly beautiful when coming off a twelve-hour flight? Well, I can't help you with that.*

What I *can* help you with are all the pro tips I've gleaned over the years from pet experts and frequent travelers when it comes to pet plane travel.

Why Are You Flying?

Before your pup puts a paw on the tarmac, ask yourself why your dog is making the trip.

Are you a regular traveler, and your dog goes where you go?

Are you moving cities/states/countries and this will be your dog's first plane experience?

Does your dog work with you and they need to accompany you in a professional capacity?

Understanding the reasons behind your trip can influence the decisions you make from here on in. Because while you certainly won't want to leave Butterscotch in Boston when you move to San Fran, you may want to look at the option of driving her cross-country. It all comes down to the individual dog.

High-Flying Hounds

It's important to know air travel can be risky for pets, but also travel can be a rewarding experience. As a dog mama, it's up to you to understand the pitfalls and benefits.

When planning your trip, first consider all the alternatives to flying. Will your dog be happier staying at home or traveling by car? Sometimes this won't be possible and it's then up to you to find the most comfortable air journey for your pupper. These days, you'll tend to have two choices:

Flying in the Cabin: When your pet needs to travel via air, always opt for them to fly in the cabin with you if possible. This allows you to be there to tend to their needs, and make the overall trip as stress-free as possible.

Flying in Cargo: If your dog is not allowed in the cabin, the other option is flying in the cargo hold. This trip can be highly stressful for many dogs, and it's a good idea to review your travel options before committing your much-loved pooch to flying in cargo.

---

* *It's probably got something to do with the fact that she flew on a private jet and didn't spend the last day crammed into a tiny seat, eating questionable food, and forcing herself to watch five back-to-back movies while drinking way too much of free airline wine, because we're getting our money's worth, thank you very much.*

THE NEW ALTERNATIVE TO CARGO?

For larger dogs, or multiple pets, it's often hard to get them accepted into the cabin–leaving a lot of pet owners in a hopeless situation.

But now, you can actually charter private jets to transport your dog in style. Yes, it all sounds very Kardashian, and is substantially more expensive than regular air travel. Yet, experts can't deny private jet travel for pups is safer and less stressful.

A great option to keep in mind if your company is transferring you overseas and footing the moving bill!

Before You Fly

If there's one thing that experts agree on, it's more longer lasting relationships from *The Bachelor* have actually been happened when the bachelor dumped the winner, and dated the runner up.*

But pet experts? They don't care about *The Bachelor***, they just want to make sure your doggo does all the things they need to stay safe before hopping on a plane.

So, before you start clicking on half-priced deals to Hawaii, here's what you need to do to get your dog sorted . . .

1. Call Yo' Vet

All pet health professionals agree, your dog needs a thorough physical before flying. You and your vet need to look at how your pup will cope with the stress and air pressure changes involves in air travel. All dogs are different and will need different travel plans to suit their age, breed, and overall wellness.

It's also important to make sure your dog's vaccinations are up to date for the entry requirements of the destination you are traveling to.

Pro Tip!

With their shortened snouts, brachycephalic dogs (such a bulldogs and pugs) are more prone to respiratory problems during air travel. The changes in air pressure and quality during a plane trip can trigger breathing complications that can have scary, sometimes fatal, outcomes. If you're traveling with these breeds, always talk to your vet prior and have a safe travel plan in place.

2. Choose Your Pet-Friendly Airline

Start your research ASAP on airlines that travel to your destination and transport pets. Look for airlines that:

- Have the most direct route possible.
- Allow you to take your dog in the cabin with you (NEVER in the overhead bins).

---

* *True story.*
** *Well, they do a little bit. They're only human, after all.*

- Have a sound track record of safely transporting pets.
- Have a nice selection of Channing Tatum movies in their in-flight entertainment system. For your dog of course.

3. Book Early

Once you've found the best airline for you and your dog, book your flights straight away. Airlines reserve just a handful of in-cabin spots per flight and you want to make sure one of them is yours!

When booking, confirm with your airline what carrier your dog will need to travel in and any other restrictions you need to know about. Triple check the carrier dimensions required, as different airlines have different under-seat dimensions. You don't want to get all the way onto the plane and find your carrier can't fit, believe me.

It's a good idea to double-check at this stage that your dog's health and vaccination records meet the airline's requirements too.

4. Prep Your Pooch

Now you know all the airline's rules and requirements, you can get your dog in on the act. Start by getting your dog used to their approved carrier (see my handy tips on page 143) and give them lots of firsthand experience traveling inside it.

Make sure your dog's ID, collar and microchip are up to date and ensure the carrier travel label with your full name, phone numbers,

Handy Hint

Opt for flights that fall outside the busiest travel times so you and your dog don't get caught up in hectic airport rushes. Plus fewer passengers = more room for you two!

permanent address, and final destination is secured safely.

Up, Up, and Away

Bon Voyage! On the day of your trip, don't feed your pooch in the hours before your flight and try to give them as much exercise as possible to tire them out for the trip ahead. For many dogs, a plane trip is a great place to catch up on a long nap! (Just like the dude that reclined his seat in front of you and snored the entire way . . .)

Don't forget a last-minute toilet stop.

Be prepared to go through security (you can hold your dog while their carrier goes through the X-ray machine), and once you're on the plane, try to relax—a calm owner equals a happy dog.

Throughout the trip, remember, you are the sole advocate for your pooch. If you see anything you don't like or have concerns for your dog's well-being or comfort, speak up. Your dog will thank you for it.

HELP! MY DOG NEEDS TO FLY CARGO

Sometimes there's no getting round it, your pup needs to fly cargo. If this is the case add these extra tips to your preparation to make your pup's experience as safe as possible:

- Inform everyone—from your booking agent to check-in staff, to the pilot and cabin crew, that your dog will be traveling in cargo. They are the people who will monitor the safe transportation of your pup, and the temperature, pressure, oxygen, and air circulation in the cargo hold—essentially they're the ones who will ensure your pup stays safe.
- Ensure your dog's travel crate adheres to regulations, including access that allows airline staff to provide supplied food and water without opening the crate.
- Always travel on the same flight as your dog and request to watch your pet being loaded and unloaded into the cargo hold. If you see anything that concerns you, report it immediately.
- Choose flights that operate during milder temperatures. Always avoid flights that operate during extreme temperatures.
- There's no such thing as too much identification. Make sure all your details are on your dog's collar and travel label. On the day of travel take a photo of your dog, and your dog inside their crate so you have a reference photo should you need it.
- A T-shirt or small blanket with your scent on it may provide comfort for your dog in their crate. However always check to make sure your dog can't get tangled or caught up in it while inside. Toys are generally not permitted.
- On arrival, immediately release your dog from their crate when you have a safe space to do so. Check them over and if there is anything wrong take them to a vet immediately. If they're just glad to see you, give them a big hug and congratulate them on gaining their wings!

How to Be a Great Hotel Guest

Friend after five drinks: Let's take our dogs to Vegas!

Me: Have you booked pet-friendly accommodation?

Friend: Nah, it'll be fine.

Narrator: It would not be fine.

Keep you and your pup out of trouble with these handy hints on how to be the best hotel guests ever—and get invited back time and time again.

Pick Pet-Friendly

As the knight in *Indiana Jones and the Last Crusade* said, "choose wisely."

When booking accommodation, always confirm with the hotel that they are pet-friendly and ask if there are any additional restrictions—such as the size of your dog. If the hotel has special "pet rooms," make sure these are the same quality as the rest of the hotel (not the murder room that's next to the trash compactor).

Always ask up front if there are any extra pet charges not included in your room rate and find out if you'll be asked for a pet deposit at check-in. If so, confirm whether it is refundable or nonrefundable to prevent any surprises.

Lastly, check what is and isn't included in your stay. Lots of amazing pet-friendly hotels now provide luxury bedding, bowls, and more for their doggo guests. Find out what they've got on offer so you're not lugging around duplicates.

Respect the Room

This is not the time to let your dog behave like a rock star.

As a good dog mama, ensure you dog uses their own dog bowls (or hotel-provided ones) and not the plates provided for the human guests. Treat the furnishings as you would your own and ensure your dog does the same.

If your dog has a toileting accident, clean it up right away (with your cleaning kit from page 138). If you can't get things back to normal, alert the front desk right away—this goes the same for scratches or any other damage your dog might do. They might be able to get cleaning staff to fix the issue easily. If you don't report it, you may find yourself liable for even more repair charges down the line (and no one wants to be paying for Susan's chihuahua's mess).

Don't Leave Them Home Alone

It was all fun and games for Kevin McCallister at the Plaza, but leaving your dog alone in a hotel room is generally discouraged, and in some hotels, strictly against hotel policy.

Put yourself in your dog's shoes—they're tired from a long journey, in unfamiliar surroundings, and their owners have just left (and taken the minibar key with them). It's the perfect recipe for barking, chewing, and general behavior hotels don't want in their guests.

If your dog must be left alone and is permitted to do so, remember to either crate them or pop the "Do Not Disturb" sign on so hotel employees won't come face-to-face with a dog they don't know.

But really, if your dog has come all this way with you, try to bring them with you when you're out and about—that's what they're there for!

Pro Tip!

Always give any hotel-provided bowls or dishes a quick wash in hot water before giving them to your dog. Hotel cleaners agree, in-room glasses and dishes are the items least likely to be cleaned thoroughly—even in 5-star hotels.

Remember, Not Everyone Likes Dogs*

Just because a hotel is pet-friendly doesn't mean all the other guests are. Excessive barking, not cleaning up your dog's waste, and having your pup off the leash are all major no-nos when staying at hotels . . . because frankly, they're super annoying for everyone else.

And I'll let you in on a little secret: a well-behaved dog will get more head pats and smiles from fellow guests.

No-Go Zones

Always check with your hotel where your dog is and isn't allowed. Obvious examples include the breakfast buffet and the gym, but pools, outdoor cafés, and other areas may be more flexible. Ensure you know where your dog can and can't go, and plan your day accordingly (just don't miss that breakfast buffet!).

Explore!

Use the local knowledge of hotel staff to find out pet-friendly places nearby. This can be as simple as the closest places to toilet your pup, or fun dog-friendly parks and cafés. Let them guide you on their local area so you and your pupper can enjoy it!

NEVER SNEAK A DOG IN

Just like the parents who try to sneak seven kids into a standard room (I see you Sandra), or college students who pack a spring break party into their twin-share, sneaking a dog into a non-pet-friendly hotel is always going to end in tears. From budget to high-end, there are so many pet-friendly hotel options these days that you can find a place for you and your pooch to stay legitimately. So there's never a need to go undercover.

---

* Who are these people?

Questions to Ask Your Pet Sitter

Every mother needs a break from her kids, and there's no exception for dog mamas!

If you've found yourself headed off on vacation, and your pooch can't come, an in-home pet sitter is often the safest, most comfortable way to care for your dog when you're gone.

Now while fourteen-year-old-Becky-who-has-read-one-chapter-of-a-Baby-Sitters-Club-book* may be fine for your neighbor's actual kids, I'd suggest going for a pet-sitting professional for your fur baby.

Here's how to find one that your dog will love (but never as much as they love you, okay?)

Get the Basics

- Do you want your pet sitter to stay at your home, or will they bring your pup to their place?
- If it's the latter, do they have other dogs, children, or family members that will be interacting with your dog? Is their space safe, secure, and large enough to accommodate your dog?
- What will your pet sitter be required to do? Daily meals and walks? Grooming? Gourmet meals? Teaching them basic Spanish? What sounds simple to you may be extravagant to someone else and vice versa!

Get a Short List

Chat to friends at the dog park, ask for recommendations on social media, and reach out to all the dog moms and dads you know to find some pet-sitter options. Ask for references, testimonials from repeat clients, and look at their social accounts to get a feel for the quality of service they provide.

Confirm that they can deliver on all the skills and attributes you require. Do they have a driver's license? Insurance? A certificate in pet first aid? How many years' experience do they have? Do they care for multiple dogs or will your dog be their sole charge? Do they have a day job that could impact their pet-sitting duties? Do they have an emergency backup plan if something happens to them?

Make sure you meet with at least two or three different minders. You'll quickly get a feel for which one best suits your fur child and will make the final decision much easier.

Last but certainly not least, watch how they interact with your dog! Does your dog immediately respond to them? Are they gentle and responsive to your dog's body language? Do they make an effort to play with your dog and show affection? Ultimately it's going to

---

* Book #3, The Truth About Stacey, *for those playing at home.*

be these two who are spending all their time together, so you want to make sure they click!

Keep the Routine

Before locking in your chosen pet sitter, ask them if they can commit to the daily regime your dog currently has.

Dogs thrive on routine, and with their mama away, even more so. If your pooch is used to regular twice-daily walks or a trip to the park, then ensure your minder is able to offer this. Same goes for their diet and grooming routine which needs to be kept while you're away.

Once you've confirmed all the details with your pet sitter, write them down and have them readily accessible. A cliff notes for you doggo if you will, this info sheet should include all your contact details, vet numbers, emergency numbers, meal info, any medications and dosages, plus daily exercise needs. That way, at a glance, your pet sitter has all the information she needs at her fingertips to be a total expert on your dog.

Love Notes

A great pet sitter will send you regular texts, messages, and photos of your dog while you're away. Chat about this before you leave so you both know how often you expect to be updated. That way you can enjoy your vacation with peace of mind that your dog is in the very best of hands.

@wtfrenchie
wheresthefrenchie.com

Travel Hacks
with Nikki Star

Nikki Star is a Los Angeles–based creative director, mom to Insta-famous Frenchies Weston + Fira, and founder of wheresthefrenchie.com: a chic blog highlighting pet-friendly travel and lifestyle.

What are your go-to dog travel tips?

Book ASAP. Most airlines fill the available in-cabin pet spots on a first-come, first-served basis and most only allow a certain number of pets on board (sometimes only two to four spots). Search for flights "incognito" or in a "private window." I've noticed prices on airline sites can fluctuate due to them tracking searches but doing it incognito gives you more assurance you're getting the best, true price.

Flying with your pet in a carrier means they become your carry-on item. Once you get on board, the carrier goes under the seat and your personal item (bag) has to go up in the overhead bin. Take advantage of those extra handy pockets in the pet carrier, so you don't have to get up mid-flight!

Sometimes flying is just not an option with your pet, so traveling by car with your dog can be a great way to see the world together. Rest stops are always great at pet stores so you can stock up on treats and use the (human) bathroom while accompanied by your pup.

Many hotels don't charge an extra fee if you travel with your pet, so save some money by picking out the pet-friendly hotels with no fees! These fees can add up, so it's always worth it to check.

What is a common mistake people often make when traveling with their pets?

I always try to pack light for myself and for the dogs.

It's always good to be over-prepared with your pets (like having extra copies of health certificates) but there's no need to pack their bowls nine out of ten times. They just add bulk to luggage. Hotels will have bowls or if you're doing something like camping, pack the collapsible bowls so you don't have the extra weight.

What are your "must-haves" when packing for dogs?

- A small collapsible water bowl.
- Nose butter! Weston and Fira's noses can get dry and crusty especially if we're flying, so an organic balm is good to have on hand. You can even use it on their paws or ears.
- Baby wipes are a must for a quick wipe down of the pups or any (oops!) pet-related accidents.
- If you're going away for more than a day or two and can find the space in your bag, try to bring your dog's favorite chew toy or two from home. It definitely makes them feel more at ease and comfortable in new places.

Always have treats! I love having all-natural, freeze-dried chicken, fish, sweet potato, or beef treats for the pups when traveling.

What are your all-time favorite pet-friendly destinations?

Close to home in California, I love the casual elegance of the Ojai Valley Inn and so do the pups; they just love exploring and running free on its 220 acres. Ojai is known for its spiritually healing grounds and mystical energy. It's definitely a must-experience spot for pet parents and fur babies alike!

In a tiny town in Idaho, there is a 30-foot beagle. Yes, a real beagle-shaped bed & breakfast built by a couple as an homage to their sweet Willy. Dog Bark Park Inn has become a famous landmark and it is *adorable*. They offer fresh baked treats for humans and pups, board games, and of course, the perfect Instagram selfie.

Just two hours north of Los Angeles, there's a gorgeous town called Montecito (where Oprah and Ellen make their homes). It's also home to the magical San Ysidro Ranch resort. During our stay here, they welcomed us with doggie biscuits with Weston's name written in peanut butter! They also print postcards with your pet's photo to take home.

Boris & Horton—the first dog café in NYC! Located in the East Village, you can come in with your pup to enjoy coffee and a yummy food menu. I wish these were everywhere!

What one item could you, as a dog mama, not live without?

My Saint Rue leash. It's shorter than most leashes out there, so it's easier to walk the dogs around when traveling without worrying about them getting tangled or straying too far. The striped design also adds an extra oomph to my outfits!

Milestones & Entertaining

How to Throw a Puppy Party

Have a special birthday coming up? Want to celebrate a special holiday with your pooch by your side? Need an excuse to drink champagne before midday? Time to throw a puppy party! The great thing about a dog lovers' meet up is you get to meet like-minded people, and your pup gets to play with other doggos to their heart's content.

These days, we're all meeting so many dog-friendly people through Instagram and Facebook, that it makes sense to take that friendship off-screen. But how to do it? It's never been easier to get your own party started . . .

The Guest List

To kick things off, you first need to decide on a guest list. Obviously being a dog lovers' meet up, you're going to have humans and hounds there.

Decide how many people you can accommodate and then invite from there. If it's your first party, the more intimate the better—save yourself the stress of an overflowing guest list.

Define your invite list. Want to connect with other dog lovers in your local area? Want a breed-specific get-together? Want to meet your Insta-friends in real life? Use social media to arrange and invite like-minded dog lovers and you've got yourself a meetup!

The Location

Once you know how many people and pups are coming, decide on a venue that can comfortably accommodate you all and make any bookings required. Local parks, dog-friendly beaches, and pet-friendly cafés make perfect puppy party venues.

Make sure there's enough space for the puppers to play, and that it's a safe space away from major obstacles. Water bowls, toilet spots, shaded areas, and access for pets are all things to think about. Don't forget to have a wet-weather plan!

For food, decor, or activities, keep it as low key or as stunningly styled as you want. Fun dog-themed snacks, decor, photobooths, goodie bags, and activities all make for a memorable event.

On the Day

- Send out social media reminders closer to the event to make sure everyone is ready or has any last-minute questions.
- Make sure you have an emergency stash of doggy waste bags and treats just in case.
- Consider inviting a few attendees to arrive early to help you set up—especially if you've got fancy decorations or lots of food to prep.
- Dress up in style! That goes for your dog too—a cute bow tie or a cool collar is the perfect icebreaker.
- Don't forget to take photos and videos—capture those memories. For more formal events consider having a designated photographer on hand.
- Last but not least, have fun! These are your people. Get to know them and their pups beyond the screen—you never know, it might be the start of a lifelong friendship.

SAFE PARTY TIPS

Make sure all the dogs on your guest list are healthy, vaccinated, play safely, and are friendly with other dogs.

If you're meeting new people for the first time, make sure you have friends with you on the day of, and inform them of the party plans, details, and invite list. No one intentionally invites a Craiglist murderer to their puppy party, but best to play it safe.

GREAT PUPPER PARTY IDEAS

Valentine's Day Party—no better time to show the real loves of your life what they mean to you.

Super Bowl Party—don't forget to watch the Puppy Bowl first!

Easter Egg Hunt—replace chocolate eggs with dog-friendly snacks.

Halloween Fancy Dress—have prizes for the best-dressed person and pooch pair!

Holiday Party—Organize a "Secret Santa" gift exchange prior so every dog gets a gift on the day.

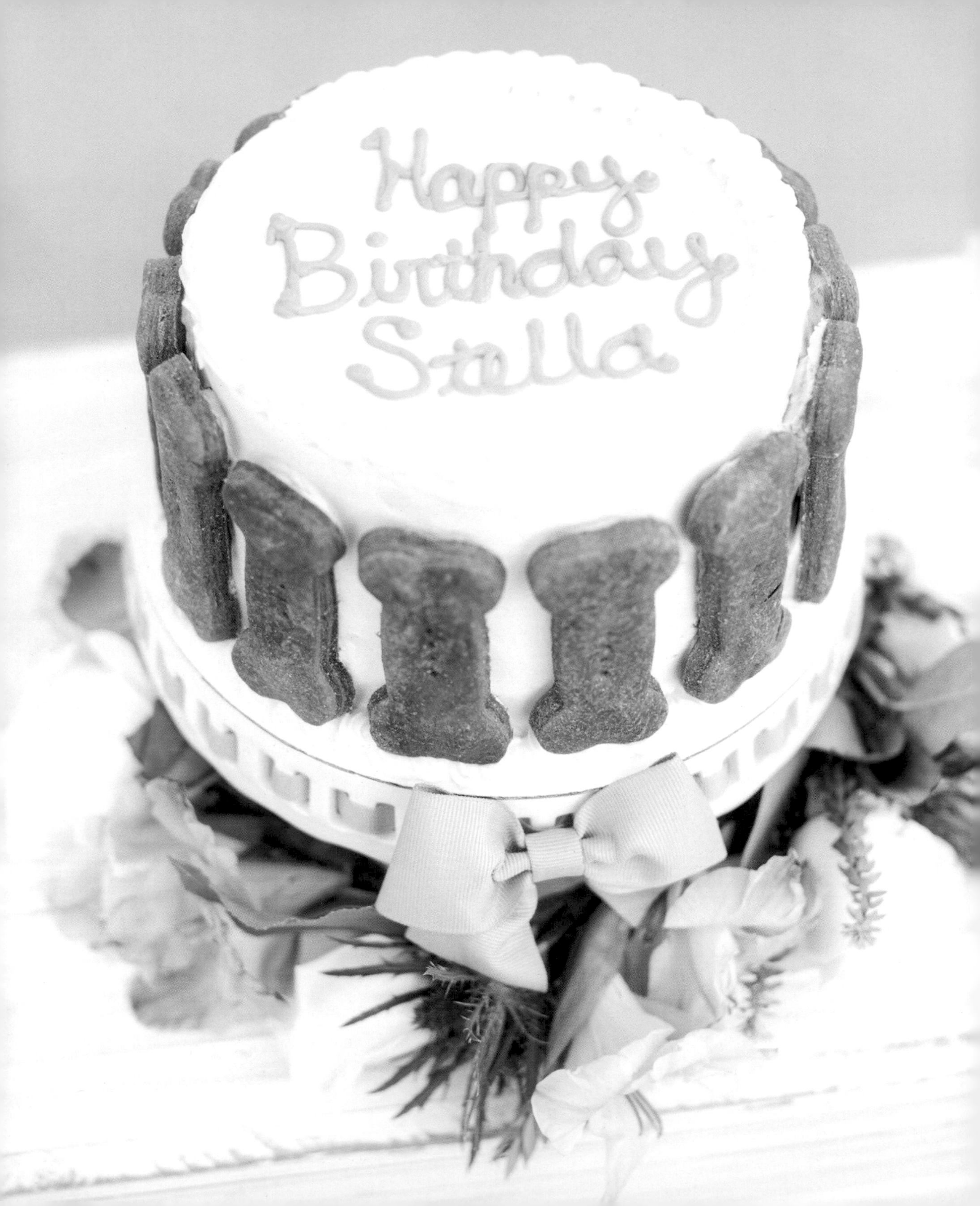
Happy
Birthday
Stella

Smash It! How to Do a Doggie Cake Smash

First they started with babies, then some fully grown adults got into the craze (let's never speak of that again . . .) But the cutest cake smashes of all time? Doggo ones.

A fun, fairly easy way to celebrate a milestone birthday, dog cake smashes combine a sweet treat with the most adorable photo opportunity. Here's how to pull off an all-time pupper cake smash you and your dog will love.

Choose Your Cake

This part can be as easy or hard as you'd like it to be. Make sure you opt for a dog-friendly cake, as human cakes are not good for dogs. Either enlist the help of your local dog bakery or make your own.

Keep in mind the size of your dog to ensure the cake is an ideal size for them to eat without getting bloated. Try to include dog-friendly frosting on your cake as it makes for a better "smash" and lots of licking shots.

Choose Your Location

Pick a location that provides a nice backdrop, a spot that has some sentimental meaning to you and your dog, and finally, an area that your know your dog will be comfortable in.

At home is an easy option, or a local garden could work as well. Off-leash dog parks are not an ideal location for cake smashes, as frankly every dog there is going to want to eat that cake. Opt for a quieter location where you'll have the space (and cake!) to yourselves.

Style Your Shot

Starting with your cake, try to keep the styling of your cake smash simple. Keep your palette to three or four colors to keep a cohesive look, and match any props or accessories to your cake.

Personalized bandanas, party hats, or bows can dress up your dog, while flower displays, balloons, or garlands can enhance the backdrop. If you opt for using candles on your cake, ensure they remain unlit and within easy reach so your dog doesn't end up eating one!

Capture the "Cake Smash" Moment

After putting together a beautifully styled shoot, the best part is finally letting your pup dig in and enjoy their cake!

For pups with amazing self-restraint, try and grab some shots of them next to the cake before they eat it. If they're really good

(or haven't figured out the cake is for them!) give them a little frosting on their snout and let them lick it off—this makes for adorable photos.

Once you give the okay to dig in, make sure you're set up and ready to take a lot of pictures in a row—that cake will disappear fast! Don't be like Uncle Jerry and have the lens cap still on your camera—you will miss it if you're not quick. That said, some dogs may need to be encouraged. Give them a taste of the frosting on your finger and let your pupper take their time with the cake.

Fun First!

Let's admit it, if we have the time and inclination to give our doggo a cake smash for their birthday . . . life is sweet. So keep it fun (for you and your pupper) and never forget—often the best photos happen when things go wrong!

If there are multiple dogs present, ensure they are all happy and have their own treats to keep them occupied while the birthday floofer enjoys their cake.

And don't forget to serve water. Keeping your pup hydrated at all times is important, especially after the cake smash and that sticky frosting.

Cleanup

Truth be told, most dogs will keep eating until there's no mess left, so cleanup for a cake smash should be relatively easy. After the last crumbs are devoured, or your dog loses interest—whichever comes first—make sure you tidy up. Having some wipes on hand to clean up any messes makes for a hassle-free event.

DIY: DOG BIRTHDAY CAKE

Cake:
- 2 tablespoons coconut oil
- 1¾ cups almond flour
- 2 tablespoons honey
- 3 eggs
- 5 small fresh strawberries, hulled and diced

Icing:
- ½ cup plain organic yogurt
- 3 tablespoons natural peanut butter

Method:
1. Preheat oven to 175°C / 345°F. Use coconut oil to grease two small ramekin dishes. Depending on the size of your dishes, you may have enough batter for 3 layers.
2. Mix flour, honey, and eggs in the blender until a smooth batter forms, then fold in the diced strawberries.
3. Pour batter into the prepared ramekin dishes, about ¾ of the way full.
4. Bake for 15 to 20 minutes, or until golden brown and a skewer comes out clean.
5. Allow cakes to cool in pan for 5 minutes and then transfer to cooling racks.
6. While your mini cakes are cooling, make your icing. Combine the yogurt and peanut butter and mix until smooth.
7. Once your cakes are completely cool, spread your icing onto the tops of each layer and stack. Drizzle the remaining icing over the top of the cake, garnish with berries of your choice, and serve.

Makes a 2–3 layer mini-cake.

How to Include Your Dog in a Wedding

Everyone knows it: dogs are the new kids, so of course they're going to be at your wedding. (In fact when I got married, our dog was allowed but no kids were! That went down well with our families . . .)

But you've gotta do it right. With the right planning and styling, a pet-friendly wedding can become the wedding of the year. Here are the expert top tips on how to include your pupper on your special day.

Know Your Dog

As much as you love your doggo, you need to decide first and foremost if a wedding is the right place for them. Are they okay in crowds? Will they try to gobble up the canapés? Can they sit quietly through the service? Have realistic expectations of your pupper and go from there.

You can always get shots of your dog with you getting ready prior to the ceremony, or a nice family photo afterward, without your dog actually having to be in attendance. Because no one wants to have their wedding immortalized as the one where the page boy got dragged down the aisle by Fluffernutter the golden retriever.

Work out what your dog is capable of and include them in a comfortable way. If you can't have your dog there on the day, consider including them in another way—such as naming a guest table or cocktail after your furry friend.

Find a Pet-Friendly Venue

Not all venues are dog-friendly, so make sure you ask before you book if you want to include your pooch.

Once you know your dog is allowed to attend, double-check with your location and vendors as to any issues that may pose a threat to your dog's safety. From toxic flowers in your bridal bouquet, to unattended food stations, ensure your dog will be kept away from anything that could harm them.

Let People Know That Your Dog Will Be a Guest of Honor

This includes your celebrant, your photographer, and any guests you know may not be comfortable around pooches. When I got married we actually introduced our wedding photographer to our dog during our engagement session, just so everyone was comfortable—including our dog.

Assign a Dog Handler for the Day

Not your hubby-to-be, your mom, or your maid of honor—they have their own jobs to do on the day! Whether it's a professional pet handler or a friend, it just needs to be someone your dog is comfortable with so you can relax knowing your pup is happy and in safe hands while you're off enjoying your day. With so many companies offering this service now, it's easy to get a carer. Whoever you choose, make sure you meet with them prior to ensure both you and your dog will be relaxed on the day.

When the big day comes, ensure they have enough treats, water, waste bags, toys, and wipes for cleanup to keep all bases covered.

Primp!

If your dog is going to be part of your big day, book them in for a groom the week prior. Make sure any accessories are planned ahead of time and blend with your overall wedding aesthetic. A simple flower on their collar, or matching bow tie can be a classic and timeless statement (see page 179 for our DIY wedding bow tie and page 181 for our DIY floral wedding wreath).

Plan Your Photos

One of the biggest drawcards for including your dog in your wedding is to have treasured photos of your furry friend at such a milestone occasion.

If there are certain shots you want with your dog on your wedding day, communicate this

to your photographer. Give them examples of photographs you like, and discuss when and where these photos can be taken on the day. That way you, your photographer, and your dog are all prepared.

Remember Why Your Dog Is There!

In the lead-up to your wedding you may have a few traditionalists say a wedding is no place for a dog. If I had collected $1 for every time someone said that my pup was going to jump on me and ruin my dress . . . well, I'd be a very wealthy dog mama. But guess what? My dog was perfectly behaved all day. If you want your dog to be part of your wedding, make no apologies for it—they are part of your family, after all, and you deserve to have them there to cheer you on.

ROLES FOR DOGS AT WEDDINGS

- Flower dog
- Ring bearer
- Best dog
- Bridesdog
- Dog of honor

Handy Hint

- Before you start, measure your dog's neck or collar size and trim the ribbon accordingly. Always give a bit of extra room to ensure your pup is comfortable on the day.
- It's important to note, this wedding bow-tie is intended to be a fun accessory for your wedding and is not recommended to be used as a collar.

DIY: No-Sew Wedding Bow Tie

Why make your own bow tie? Why, it's as simple as saving money* and also you can match the exact fabric to your wedding party!

Timeless, elegant, and super easy, this DIY can be made in minutes and will feature in photos for years to come (giving you more time to go over that seating chart and work out where in the world you're going to stick Aunty Gladys . . .).

You'll Need:

- Fabric
- Scissors
- Thick velvet ribbon
- Velcro squares—the ones with the sticky backs

Method:

1. Cut your fabric to approximately 4 x 9 inches. This is a standard size for a dog bow tie, but if you are making this for large and extra-large pups, increase the size. Cut a second skinny strip of fabric approximately 2 x 5 inches.
2. Take your large fabric piece and fold into thirds lengthways, with the top and bottom sides overlapping slightly.
3. Fold in the left and right sides crossways. Dependant on your desired bow tie length, choose how much you want the left and right sides to overlap.
4. Pinch the center of the folded fabric with your fingers to make a bow shape.
5. Using your skinny piece of fabric, tie around the center of the bow. Make sure the knot is tight and secure. Trim the excess from the knot.
6. Take your ribbon, and add a Velcro square (the one with the scratchy side) to the center and to the far right end of the ribbon length. On the left end of the ribbon add a fuzzy Velcro square to the back side. Using another fuzzy Velcro square, add one to the back of the bow.
7. Stick the bow to the center of the ribbon. Attach the ends together and you have a stunning dog bow tie ready for the big day!

_____

* *Money that can be better spent at a swim-up bar in the Maldives #honeymoon.*

Safety First!

When choosing your flowers for your wreath, please be aware that a number of flowers can be toxic if ingested by dogs. Although your dog wedding wreath is obviously not for consumption, if you have concerns your dog may eat or chew at the wreath, please err on the side of using 100 percent nontoxic plants. Always keep your dog under supervision while wearing the wreath.

DIY: Floral Wedding Wreath

The perfect statement piece for a beautiful wedding, this floral wreath will make your dog the center of attention . . . except of course when they're looking at you—you know, the actual bride.

You'll Need:
- 2–3 bouquets of any nonirritant, flexible stemmed flower
- Scissors
- Floral tape
- Floral wire

Method:

1. Lay out your flowers and begin separating them. Using your scissors, begin cutting off branched groupings of flowers. Once you have your bouquet cut into individual branches, lay them out on a flat surface and begin grouping/bunching them in a vertical line with the stems overlapping one another.

2. Use your floral tape to join and secure the stems together, and wrap floral wire around any spots that need extra support or that have little flyaway pieces. As you add flowers, it should start to resemble a garland.

3. Once your garland is long enough to hang loosely around your dog's neck, join the ends together by overlapping them and securing them with wire/tape. Overlapping the pieces will disguise the tips and give it a smoother finish. Gently place the wreath over your dog's head so that it hangs comfortably for photos.

How to Prepare Your Dog for a Baby (A Dog Lovers' Guide)

Regular Moms: It's just a dog . . .
Dog Mamas: First of all, that's my child.

Google "how to prepare your dog for a baby" and you'll get an infinite number of responses. Trouble is, a lot of these so-called "guides" are written by baby and "mommy" sites which have all the focus on the newborn and pretty much treat the dog like a troublesome piece of furniture. Seriously.

But guess what? It's the twenty-first century, and dog mamas like us are having none of that. Having a baby is the start of a whole new world for you and your family—and that includes your dog. If you are expecting, and want a happy and healthy environment for your new baby, your family, *and* your pooch, here's what you need to do.

Call in Reinforcements

They say raising a child takes a village. And guess what? That extends to our furry children. The first thing you can do when preparing your dog, and your family, for a baby is to give your dog a backup family. This can be a close friend or family member who can develop a bond with your dog during your pregnancy, and also has the resources to care for them in their own home if needed. A home away from home, if you will.

Why do you need a backup family? Because not all pregnancies and births go as planned. High-risk pregnancies happen, and babies can arrive early or with special medical needs meaning you can end up practically living at the hospital for weeks on end.*

Even if everything goes smoothly, having a newborn is a whole new experience. You need to be kind to yourself, give yourself time to heal, and bond with your baby. Giving your dog another person they see as family, and a second home to go to, allows you peace of mind during this time and ensures your dog always feels loved.

DO approach any potential friends or family with this proposal as soon as you can. This

---

* *In fact, when I was writing this very book I gave birth seven weeks early. Surprise! Lucky for us, our dog Butters was more than happy to head to his Nan and Pop's house for a short vacation while I was in hospital—or as he calls it "the land of endless walks and treats."*

gives your dog time to get to know them and have some trial visits and sleepovers at their place to ensure they are comfortable. In many cases your dog will start seeing their backup family as a fun vacation!

DO ensure your dog has a good advance supply of pet food, treats, and any medications they are on. Make sure they are also up to date with all vaccinations as well.

DON'T treat your backup family as a replacement home for your pet. Remember your dog's favorite place is with you, in your home.

Work It Out

The number one thing you can do to keep your dog happy, healthy, and calm during the arrival of your new baby? A daily walk.

You can buy your dog every dog treat, toy, and fancy collar under the sun, but without a daily outlet to release their energy and get outside, even the best dogs become depressed, destructive, and start sporting some serious eyeliner.

While looking after a newborn, *and* taking your dog for a walk seems like mission impossible (not to mention factoring in some actual sleep), with a little bit of planning it can be done. As soon as you find out you're expecting, follow this guide:

DO start to vary the times of walks and outings. That way while your dog still gets their daily walk, they don't get into a routine of expecting at a certain time of day. Because really, if you've been up with a baby all night, is Bella the Border Collie's 6:00 a.m. walk time going to sound that appealing?

DO start to vary who goes on walks and outings. Don't leave the dog walking up to one family member. Your pup needs to learn to be comfortable being taken out by a number of people. That way when one of you is occupied, the other one can step in and go for the walk.

DO consider enrolling your dog in doggie day care or enlisting a local dog walker to help out if it all seems too much. Knowing your dog is enjoying her time away from the house will do you both good.

DON'T wing it. Make a plan of how you are going to keep up your dog's regular activity and stick to it. This is nonnegotiable. A well-exercised dog is a happy dog.

Go Back to School

If up until this point, your household has had a laissez-faire attitude to rules, it's time to make a change. Don't go all Aunt-Lydia-*Handmaid's-Tale* on us, but just step it up a notch.

Once you find out you're pregnant, there's no better time to teach or reinforce your dog's basic training and understanding of house rules. By clearly making it known that you're the pack leader, your dog will feel secure in their place in the pack when the baby comes. *Blessed be the fruit.*

DO ensure your dog understands basic commands such as sit, drop, and stay. Enlist a dog trainer's help if necessary, as these commands will be invaluable when you're introducing fur-child number one to human-child number two. When training, always use positive reinforcement methods such as treats and praise. This will not only get the best results, but it will strengthen the bond between you and your pup.

DO clearly define any "off-limit" zones in the house prior to the baby's arrival. If the nursery is to be a no-go zone, get your dog used to this months before your due date. That way your dog will not associate being excluded with the presence of the baby.

DON'T introduce new rules when you bring the baby home. Like the "off-limit" zones, work on these new boundaries during your pregnancy. If your dog will no longer be allowed on the furniture, or discouraged from jumping up, teach them these new rules prior to the baby's arrival.

Prep, Prep, Prep

With a new baby, your dog is going to be bombarded with a whole truckload of new smells, sounds, and experiences. By preparing your pup and introducing these to your dog in a gradual way, you can help prevent an all-out assault on their senses when the baby first comes home.

DO get your dog used to the sounds a new baby will make. Use a recording from YouTube, or borrow a real baby (send their mom off for a massage and she'll love you forever), then watch how your dog reacts to all the different sounds. Pretty much, within anything from a couple of minutes to an hour, most dogs will reach a point of giving zero f*cks—funnily enough, while you will come to hate these noises and question all of your life choices.

DO let them sniff some of the baby's things. When you're in the hospital, send home a blanket or wrap that has your baby's scent on it. Get your dog to sit calmly and then allow them to sniff the item. This allows them to get used to the new smell, while also associating their calm behavior with the scent.

DON'T bombard them with baby gadgets in one go. In the lead-up to birth, allow your dog to see the new baby gear up close and personal. Wheel the stroller around, fill up the baby bath, turn the baby swing on . . . whatever you are planning on using when the baby comes home, get your dog used to it beforehand. The last thing you want is your dog chasing the stroller wheels on baby's first outing!

DO reorganized your car, to ensure it can fit your baby's car seat, and a safe space for your dog, ensuring they are safely separated.

Keep Calm

During pregnancy and the lead-up to birth, things can get very stressful very quickly. It's a whole new adventure for all of you.

By promoting a safe and calm space within the home, you will ensure not only your dog remains happy and healthy, but the whole family does.

DO provide a safe, warm space for your dog to curl up in away from the baby. Knowing they have this space to themselves will offer them a retreat if needed.

DON'T decide now is the time to move your indoor dog to being an outdoor dog. Your dog is a pack animal and banishing them outdoors to make room for a new baby will make them feel alone and confused.

DON'T raise your voice at your dog when stressed. Your dog will pick up on your stress levels and internalize your stress. If you're frustrated or upset, leave the room and take a few deep breaths. Rely on your dog's training, use positive reinforcement in a calm manner, and you'll encourage calm behavior in your dog.

At the Birth

You never know when a baby is going to decide to turn up! But the last thing you want is the whole family rushing off in the middle of the night and no one returning for days, leaving pooch all alone.

DO have a plan. Before you pack your hospital bag, plan who is going to care for your dog while you're in hospital (a great time to call on your backup family!). Don't make it Cousin Gary who flakes on everything. Make sure they know all the requirements for caring for your dog, including emergency contacts.

DON'T enlist the help of a stranger. Ensure whoever is going to look after your dog comes over and gets to know your dog prior to caring for them. Make sure they are comfortable on walks and with feeding. That way your dog will welcome them with open arms when they come at the time of the birth.

DO greet your dog as normal when you return home—don't have your focus all on the new baby. Your dog has missed you while you've been away, and returning home just like it's a regular day will keep things as normal and calm as possible.

INTRODUCING YOUR BABY

- Introduce your new baby to your dog at a time when everyone is relaxed and calm. After your dog comes home from a walk is ideal. Ensure you have a second adult present who can help remove your pup from the situation if required.
- Allow your dog to approach you and the baby at their own pace. Never force a dog to meet a baby. Let them smell the baby's feet while you reassure them and positively reinforce calm behavior with praise.
- Repeat this process over the first few weeks until your dog's overall curiosity declines.
- If your dog shows uncomfortable or aggressive behavior around your new baby, seek professional advice.

Remember . . . You're a Dog Mama, Too

For a lot of dogs, they came first. Many were on the scene long before any partners or children came along. Remember, they didn't judge you that time you sat on the couch for an entire weekend watching *Golden Girls* reruns, and eating nothing but donuts. Girl, they know your secrets.

While you're now a baby mama and your time is limited, it's important to carve out alone time with your dog on a regular basis to keep the bond between the two of you strong.

DO spend quality one-on-one time with your dog every day. This is not only for their benefit, but yours too. Some time out together—even just cuddle watching *The Crown*, or a short game of fetch, will recharge you both, promoting a happy healthy family for everyone.

Pro Tips for a Pet-Friendly Nursery

When you're a dog mama who's about to become a baby mama, it's important to create a space that is not only safe and comforting to your new two-legged addition, but mindful of your fur child's needs and limitations as well.

So in between buying blankets, baby moccasins, and bunny rugs, grab these goodies to make life easier for your future self.

Puppy Rug

This one is a no-brainer if you're allowing your doggo inside the baby's room. Simply a comfy mat or rug, it becomes your dog's safe space when they are invited into the nursery. During your pregnancy, take the time to train your pupper to "go to the mat" on command. This gives them a clear space where they can safely sit or lie down without being banished from the nursery. With your doggo safely on their mat, it then allows you the freedom to move about, nurse, rock, and play without tripping over your pup or having them jump up at an inappropriate time.

Smart Storage

Opt for drawer storage or closed baskets for baby's items. Open shelving holding clothing, wraps, nappies, and baby goodies on your dog's level can prove just a little too enticing. The same goes for not having an open toy basket. After years of your pup having the only toy bin in the house, introducing a new basket full of plush, squeaky toys can be an invitation for trouble!

As your child grows up, your dog will soon learn to differentiate between their things and the baby's, yet by putting these design elements in place, it just makes things easier for everyone in those early, dazed and confused months.

Diaper Pail

Dogs and dirty diapers do not mix. Lock that sh*t away.

Baby Gate

A retractable baby gate is the perfect solution for times where your pup needs to be outside the nursery. Retractable gates fit seamlessly into their surroundings, and offer flexibility for when you need your pup and baby to be separated.

Pet Memorials

As much as no one likes to talk about it, the sad reality of having our dogs in our lives is the fact that there will come a time where we will have to say goodbye to them.

The heartbreak of losing a beloved pet and then missing them for years on end is extremely hard. But knowing that you honored them and their memory gives you so much peace as a dog mama.

There are so many beautiful memorial concepts now that allow you to respect your dog at the time of their passing and honor them in a way that treasures their soul for the years to come.

It's a good idea to look at these ideas, even if your pup is a strapping, healthy doggo barking at the cat across the street right now. Knowing what options you have and how you'd like to remember your pet makes it so much easier when the time comes to say goodbye.

Pet Burial and Farewell Kits

One of the hardest parts of saying goodbye is farewelling your dog's physical body. The same body that has snuggled up to you on the couch, hounded you for one more throw of the ball, and been a constant presence in your home. How do you say goodbye?

Pet burial and farewell kits allow your departed best friend to rest peacefully and snugly before burial or cremation. They are a beautiful last act of respect and kindness to your much-loved pup.

There are a number of options available, however two farewell kits that I personally admire include:

Sweet Goodbye (sweetgoodbye.com.au, available at Amazon.com) cocoons allow your dog to be gently enfolded within thick layers of hand-woven wool, snug and secure for their final resting place. The unique, environmentally friendly registered design includes a built-in carrying cradle, to make lifting and carrying safe and easy for you while keeping your pet protected and secure during transportation. Each kit comes with everything you need at the final stage to plan a ceremony at home or with your veterinarian and prepare a beloved pet for their final journey.

Orchard Valley Forever Beds (orchidvalley petcaskets.com.au, available at Amazon.com) are tasteful, eco-friendly pet caskets suitable for natural burial or cremation. They come with a complimentary temporary grave marker and photograph frame and provide a dignified and respectful option for your dog, that in turn gives much peace to you at a heartbreaking time.

A Heartfelt Tattoo

One of the most popular ways to pay tribute to a beloved pet is to get a tattoo.

Whether it's a full portrait of your pup or a simple quote or paw print, there's no better way to have your dog become part of you forever.

Custom Charms

A custom charm featuring your dog's name, paw print, or nose imprint is a subtle, yet heartfelt way to carry your dog in your heart on a daily basis. With a number of artisans online offering these services, it's a great way to treasure your dog forever.

One charm brand I personally have used and loved is **silhouPETte** (silhoupette.com) Their one-of-a-kind, hand-crafted charm necklaces feature your dog's very own silhouette. You simply send in your photo and they create a bespoke necklace with your dog's own features. Their beautiful, understated designs mean you can wear your memorial necklace for years to come, close to your heart.

Etchings, Bespoke Illustrations, and Photo Books

My dear friend and dog mama, Sarah Dickerson, gifted me a photo book at the time of my beloved dog Soda's passing. It remains one of my most treasured possessions to this day.

Filled with beautiful photos of your treasured pet, and the option to include inspirational quotes, these books are a beautiful tribute to help you remember your pet and the good times you shared.

I'll often read Soda's photo book to my daughter before she goes to sleep. It's a wonderful way to remember much-loved dogs forever.

Etchings, custom pet portraits, and illustrations are also another beautiful, creative way to keep your dog's memory alive in your home.

Memorial Plants

Possibly the most beautiful and long-lasting way to treasure your pet is with a memorial plant. I have known people to grow everything from giant oak trees to a small display of flowers in memory of their loved dogs.

Choose a plant that is sturdy, easy to care for, and suitable for your lifestyle.

While seeds may seem like a small memorial at the time, they will grow to become a beautiful living memorial for your beloved pet.

Entertaining with Pets
with Abby Capalbo

Abby Capalbo is an editorial stylist based in Rhode Island with a love for perfectly imperfect and under-styled lifestyle imagery. Her affinity for finding beauty in the simple moments and her appreciation for everyday beauty is a main driver in all her styling work. Her two golden retrievers, Otto and Clementine, are often featured throughout her work and are a major inspiration to constantly be present. Her work has been featured on *Style Me Pretty Living*, *Domino*, *Real Simple*, *Country Living*, *Southern Living Magazine*, and *One Kings Lane*, and can also be found on abbycapalbo.com

---

What are your top tips for entertaining with pets?

Be Flexible.

I think this pertains to entertaining in general, but it really applies when pets are involved. Pets can be unpredictable (Otto, I'm talking to you), but some of those unpredictable moments make the best icebreakers.

I swear Otto always knows when the party needs a little life—he's got amazing comedic timing. But he's also a hooligan, and he once stole an entire block of cheese off a beautiful cheese plate we set out for guests. We all just laughed (and chased him around the house), and it's still a story we tell to this day. Lesson learned!

A "perfect" party takes on an entire new meaning with dogs involved!

Store food out of dogs' reach!

Don't set your dogs up for failure. Otto and Clemmie both know not to jump on counters or steal people food—but a party brings on a whole new level of stimulation. It's best if they aren't even tempted.

Take the party outdoors.

Give them space to "get their wiggles out," as we like to say. This also gives your dog-loving guests something to do! Put a little basket out of items the pups can fetch and everyone is entertained.

Think like a dog.

Remember, this is a big change from their day-to-day life in their home. It's a lot for most dogs, and sometimes they do better with a little break or two from the action. Stay in tune with them throughout the party, and maybe give them some time in "their place" away from the activity every once in awhile.

Reward good behavior.

Being a hostess can mean you are here, there, and everywhere—but don't forget to sneak in a snuggle with your four-legged friend during all the hustle and bustle to thank them for their behavior—in their mind, they are playing hostess too!

What are your favorite ideas for pet- and family-friendly get-togethers?

Anything outdoors! We like to bring the parties outside even in the winter months (there is nothing like a snowy bonfire), but once the weather warms up the options are endless.

From BBQs to a movie night outside (complete with puppy cuddles) or a wine tasting—being outside is good for everyone's soul.

What one item could you, as a dog mama, not live without?

Hands down, our cordless Dyson vacuum. With two golden retrievers running around, it's worth its weight in gold.

The Dog Directory

Over the last twenty years I have seen a lot of pet products. A LOT. Much dog toys. Many bandanas. Wow such collars.

The brands and boutiques listed here are the ones I trust and love. They not only have safe, durable, and stylish pet products; but they consistently impress me with their innovation in developing and creating new products for dogs to love.

What to Look for in Quality Dog Products

- Durable Materials—Look for strong rubber for chew toys, multilayered fabrics or felt wool for plush toys, and natural cotton for rope toys. For beds, look for quality foam fillings and durable outer layers. For collars, leashes, and harnesses, focus on stainless steel or solid brass hardware that won't tarnish or rust, and supple fabric or leather materials.
- Quality Construction—Look for strong, thick stitching (inversed and Z stitching for toys), strong joinery, and no small pieces that could be easily broken off and ingested.
- Machine washable or easily hand washable.
- Nontoxic—Try to avoid BPAs, PVC, phthalates, and unsafe dyes—they can be just as harmful to our pets as they are to us. For grooming products opt for natural products with no parabens, sulphates, or artificial dyes and fragrances.
- Tested to meet health and safety standards.
- Innovative and unique designs that provide comfort and/or enrichment for your dog. Pet products should be useful, fun, and stylish.

Pro Tip!

Seen that dog collar or toy you've lusted after now has a knock off version at your local big box store? Tread carefully, dog mama. While cheaper versions of your fave dog products may look almost identical, there's a few problems with purchasing them for your pupper.

First, they're often cheaper because they use lower-quality materials and construction in comparison to the originals, meaning their durability and safety can be compromised (unless you want a dog toy that's going to fall apart in your dog's mouth in a week's time?).

Secondly, by buying the copycat design you're forgetting to support the original creators. If we, as dog owners, don't support the brands that are creating original, quality pet products, these brands won't be able to compete and could very well die out. Leaving us with no more cute new designs or innovative products.

So, if you see a high-quality dog product on Instagram or in a pet store and then see a cheaper knock-off version elsewhere, for the sake of the original designer and your dog, choose the higher-quality one.

Beds & Blankets

Cloud 7 (cloud7.de/en/)

For the Furry (forthefurry.com)

FuzzYard (fuzzyard.com/us)

Harry Barker (harrybarker.com)

Labbvenn (labbvenn.com/en/)

Lion + Wolf (lionandwolf.co)

Max Bone (max-bone.com)

MiaCara (miacara.com/en/)

Mister Woof (misterwoof.net)

Modern Beast (modernbeast.com)

Molly Barker (mollybarker.com.au)

Mungo & Maud (mungoandmaud.com)

Nice Digs (nicedigs.com.au)

Pipolli (pipolli.com)

P.L.A.Y. (petplay.com)

The Foggy Dog (thefoggydog.com)

Top Dog Boutique (topdogboutique.com.au)

Waggo (waggo.com)

Bowls & Feeding

Benji & Moon (benjiandmoon.co.za)

Cloud 7 (cloud7.de/en/)

Dog Love Repeat (dogloverepeat.com)

For the Furry (forthefurry.com)

Furf Pets (furfpets.com.au)

FuzzYard (fuzzyard.com/us)

Harry Barker (harrybarker.com)

Labbvenn (labbvenn.com/en/)

Max Bone (max-bone.com)

Mungo & Maud (mungoandmaud.com)

Top Dog Boutique (topdogboutique.com.au)

Trendy Pet (trendypet.com)

Waggo (waggo.com)

Collars, Leashes & Harnesses

Barker & Bone (barkerandbone.com.au)

Benji & Moon (benjiandmoon.co.za)

Big & Little Dogs (bigandlittledogs.com)

Blanket ID (blanketid.com)

BOco (boco.com.au)

Cloud 7 (cloud7.de/en/)

Danes & Divas (danesanddivas.com)

Dizzy Dog Collars (dizzydogcollars.com)

DOGUE (dogue.com.au)

DOOG (doogusa.com)

Fetch & Follow (fetchandfollow.co.uk)

For the Furry (forthefurry.com)

FuzzYard (fuzzyard.com/us)

Harry Barker (harrybarker.com)

Haus of Harley (hausofharley.com)

Hound (houndcollection.com)

IdPet (idpet.com.au)

Ike & Stella (etsy.com/shop/ikeandstella)

Max Bone (max-bone.com)

Mister Woof (misterwoof.net)

Molly Barker (mollybarker.com.au)

Mungo & Maud (mungoandmaud.com)

My Pupper (mypupper.com.au)

Nice Digs (nicedigs.com.au)

Pablo & Co. (pabloandco.net)

Pipolli (pipolli.com)

Pupstyle (pupstylestore.com.au)

Saint Rue (saintrue.com)

Sebastian Says (sebastiansays.com.au)

See Scout Sleep (seescoutsleep.com)

Shed (shedbrooklyn.dog)

The Daily Edited (thedailyedited.com)

The Foggy Dog (thefoggydog.com)

Tommy & Bella (tommybella.com)

Top Dog Boutique (topdogboutique.com.au)

Two Tails Pet Company (twotailspetcompany.com)

Wolfpack NYC (wolfpacknyc.com)

Carriers

Cloud 7 (cloud7.de/en/)

Mungo & Maud (mungoandmaud.com)

Sleepypod (sleepypod.com)

Teddy Maximus (teddymaximus.com)

Grooming

Bondi Wash (bondiwash.com.au)

Dr Zoo (drzoo.com.au)

Essential Dog (essentialdog.com.au)

For the Furry (forthefurry.com)

FuzzYard (fuzzyard.com/us)

Harry Barker (harrybarker.com)

Houndztooth (houndztooth.com.au)

Kin + Kind (kin-kind.com)

Loyal Canine Co. (loyalcanineco.com)

Molly Barker (mollybarker.com.au)

Mr Fluff (mrfluff.com.au)

Mungo & Maud (mungoandmaud.com)

Organic Pet Company (organicpetco.com.au)

PAW by Blackmores (blackmores.com.au/paw-by-blackmores)

The Base Collective (thebasecollective.com.au/collections/pet)

Top Dog Boutique (topdogboutique.com.au)

Fashion Apparel & Accessories

Ari & M (ariandm.com)

Cloud 7 (cloud7.de/en/)

Danes & Divas (danesanddivas.com)

For the Furry (forthefurry.com)

FuzzYard (fuzzyard.com/us)

Gnocchi & Goma (gnocchiandgoma.com)

Max Bone (max-bone.com)

Mister Woof (misterwoof.net)

Mungo & Maud (mungoandmaud.com)

My Pupper (mypupper.com.au)

Pablo & Co. (pabloandco.net)

Pethaus (pethaus.com.au)

Pipolli (pipolli.com)

Ripley & Rue (ripleyandrue.com)

Sebastian Says (sebastiansays.com.au)

TailsnSails (etsy.com/shop/TailsnSails)

The Foggy Dog (thefoggydog.com)

Two Tails Pet Company (twotailspetcompany.com)

Toys

DOOG (doogusa.com)

Harry Barker (harrybarker.com)

Kong (kongcompany.com)

Modern Beast (modernbeast.com)

Molly Barker (mollybarker.com.au)

Mungo & Maud (mungoandmaud.com)

Nina Ottosson (nina-ottosson.com)

Planet Dog (planetdog.com)

P.L.A.Y. (petplay.com)

The Foggy Dog (thefoggydog.com)

Up Dog Toys (updogtoys.com)

Waggo (waggo.com)

Zippy Paws (zippypaws.com)

Pet Tech

Furbo (shopus.furbo.com)

iFetch (goifetch.com)

@jenkoala, @zippypaws
www.zippypaws.com

Choosing Quality Pet Products

with Jen Glaser

Jen Glaser is the talented cofounder and designer of ZippyPaws, the inherently popular dog toy company for the modern dog and dog owner, featuring beautifully designed, high-quality dog toys. From the conception of the brand, Jen hand-draws all of the ZippyPaws toys designs personally and brings them to life for pups all around the world to enjoy.

In the pet-parenting boom over the last decade we've seen the rise of the "dog mom." How have these stylish, smart, influential women changed the pet industry?

As more women embrace the role of "dog mom," we see a huge shift in the industry that raises the standards of pet supplies.

This customer base demands higher quality items for their fur-babies and is no longer satisfied with the low-quality, cheap products that have been saturating the market for years.

These women are raising the bar for what is considered safe for pets. And why shouldn't we? There are standards for what is safe for children, and our pets deserve that as well.

When purchasing quality pet products, what should dog owners be looking for?

In general, the best indication of a quality dog toy is the material and workmanship, such as stitching in the seams and attention to detail. To see if the material of a dog toy is high quality, touch the fabric and look at the material in detail.

Does the fluff of a plush toy come off when you pinch the material? Fluff should not come off when pinched. Does the fabric feel thick between your fingers? The material should feel thick and strong, not thin and flimsy. Can you see visible threads and sewing ends? Badly sewn seams are the first place that a dog will attack on a toy. All ZippyPaws toys are sewn so that if an extremity is chewed off (because let's be honest, the ears and arms are the most fun parts of a toy!), the rest of the toy still stays intact. Does the squeaker sound tired and thin? ZippyPaws squeakers have a minimum squeaker thickness, so that all of our squeakers are loud and durable for maximum fun for dogs and maximum annoyance for dog mamas when watching Netflix.

There are so many cheap pet products available at big box stores these days. They look like designer pet goods, but how are they different?

Usually it's pretty easy to tell when the "designer" toys at the big box stores are low-quality when you inspect the materials used. These items seem high-end because they tend to have a cohesive trendy color scheme to make them look like part of a collection. While not all products are bad, these items will be lower in quality than say, a ZippyPaws toy at the same price, because part of the proceeds will be given to a celebrity endorser or they have much more overhead. ZippyPaws toys are all designed in-house so we never have to pay designer fees, licensing fees, etc. More of our toys' cost goes toward quality materials and labor.

What five items do you think every dog mama should have for their dog?

1. A beautiful collar and leash set that reflects the individual personalities of the dog and dog mama.
2. A comfortable yet stylish dog bed that fits the chic homes of our amazing dog mamas. I personally love our dog bed by The Foggy Dog.
3. Nutritious and healthy food and treats.
4. Bully sticks. They're a nutritious chew treat that are easily digestible and keeps dogs busy for a while so you, the dog

mama, can get some calm relaxation time!
5. Toys! Of course I'm biased but toys are great for bonding through playtime.

How does your own dog influence your pet brand?

ZippyPaws was inspired by my late golden retriever JJ, who passed in 2014. He has influenced my company immensely because I wanted to make toys that would embody his fun, lively, and colorful way of life. He was the original toy tester that helped me to launch our brand. I met my fiancé the same month that JJ passed away, and his dog Kramer quickly became my own as well.

All of our team members are dog lovers and share the same values as me about treating their pets like family.

We always strive to give the best customer service, whether to consumers, our Instagram followers, or our wholesale clients. It's all about being kind to others and creating products that help families bond with their pets.

What one item could you, as a dog mama, not live without?

A camera and social media! My pup, Kramer, has his own Instagram and it helps his fans and followers to connect with him and keep up with his ever-changing hairdos.

Credits

The 6 Types of Dog Moms (p. 2-13)
Copyright © 2019 Riley Sheehey.
Illustrations used with permission of Riley
Sheehey (rileysheehey.com)

**Contents (p. ix), Introduction (p. xi), Setting
Up the Perfect Pet-Friendly Home (p. 16-21),
Pet-Proofing Like a Pro (p. 24), How to Stay
Pet-Hair Free (p. 28-33), Organizing with Pets
(p. 34-43), Grooming Like a Boss (p. 76-85),
DIY: Natural Dog Shampoo & Spray (p. 86),
Your Year Round At-Home Health Cheat Sheet
(p.88), DIY: Pet First Aid Kit (p. 91), Camera
Basics (p. 98-101), Jet-Setting Pet Tips (p. 146-
151), How to Be a Great Hotel Guest (p. 152-153),
Questions to Ask Your Pet Sitter (p. 156-159),
The Dog Directory (p. 203), Thank you (p. 212)**
Photography by Alexander Mayes Photography
(alexandermayesphotography.com)
Shot on location at "House 8" by Three Birds
Renovations (threebirdsrenovations.com)
Additional styling by Serena Faber-Nelson
(prettyfluffy.com)
Models: Lauren & Indiana (@indiana
_miniaussie), Georgia & Jerry (@littlejerryboy)
Additional pet products and props supplied by:
Dyson (dyson.com)
For the Furry (forthefurry.com)
Mister Woof (misterwoof.net)
P.L.AY. Australia (petplayaustralia.com)
The Foggy Dog (thefoggydog.com)
Two Tails Pet Company (twotailspetcompany.com)
Zippy Paws (zippypaws.com)

**DIY: Paw Print Wall Art (p. 22-23), DIY:
Toy Baskets (p. 44-45), DIY: Doggy Photo
Accessories (p. 112-113), DIY: My Dog Is Home
Alone Card (p. 144-145), DIY: Dog Birthday Cake
(p. 173), DIY: No-Sew Wedding Bow Tie (p. 178-
179), DIY: Floral Wedding Wreath (p. 180-181)**
Additional project development, styling and
photography by Sarah Dickerson
(@chicsprinkles)

**Dog Food Storage (p. 37-39), Cleaning with
Dogs (p. 46-49), DIY: All-Natural Doggy
Deodorizer (p. 51), Superfoods for Dogs
(p. 58), Fruits for Dogs (p. 62-64), DIY:
Superfood No-Bake Bliss Balls (p. 66-67),
Healthy Herbs for Your Hound (p. 68-69),
Healthy Snack Alternatives (p. 72-75), Choosing
Pet-Friendly Vacation Stays (p.134-137), Car
Travel 101 (p.138-141)**
Styling and photography by Serena Faber-
Nelson (prettyfluffy.com)
Additional props supplied by:
The Botanical Life Co (thebotanicallifeco.com.au)

Pet Friendly Plants (p.27), Pet Memorials (p.192-193)
Concept and styling by Anna Jill (kissfromfleur.de)
Photography by Bina Terré (binaterre.com)

**Apartment Living with Stephanie Sterjovski
Jolly (p. 52-55)**
Styling by Stephanie Sterjovski Jolly
(stephaniesterjovski.com)
Photography by Neal Jolly

Holistic Remedies with Sarah Dickerson (p. 92-95)

Styling and photography by Sarah Dickerson (@chicsprinkles)

How to Get Your Dog to Look at the Camera (p. 102-107)

Photography by Lauren Dobish Photography (@laurendobish, laurendobishphotography .com)

Models: Knox, Bear, Harper (@knoxandbear)

At-Home Photography (p. 108-109)

Styling and photography by Serena Faber-Nelson (prettyfluffy.com)

Models: Ollie (@ollieriver), Akela (@akelablues)

Pet Fashion with Maitri Mody (p. 114-117)

Styling and photography by Maitri Mody (honeyidressedthepug.com)

How to Choose a Pet Photographer (p. 118-121)

Photography by Lauren Dobish Photography (@laurendobish, laurendobishphotography .com)

Model: Gill (@gill_thegolden)

Prep Like a Pro—Getting Ready for a Professional Photoshoot (p.122-124)

Photography by Lauren Dobish Photography (@laurendobish, laurendobishphotography.com)

Model: Charlie (@dood_itscharlie)

Pet Coordinator: For the Love of Paws (@fortheloveofpawsss, fortheloveofpawsboston .com)

Planning + Design: Events By Carianne (@eventsbycarianne, eventsbycarianne.com)

Makeup: Sarah Lord Makeup Artist (@makeupbysarah.lord, makeupbysarahlord.com)

Hair: Styles By Callie (@stylesbycallie, stylesbycallie.com)

Florist: The Frugal Flower (@frugalflowers, frugalflower.com)

Photographing Puppies (p.125-126)

Additional research and photography by Lauren Dobish Photography (@laurendobish, laurendobishphotography.com)

Models: Puppies (@thelabslife)

Floral Crowns: Central Square Florist (@centralsquareflorist, centralsquareflorist.com)

Scarves and bows: Tails & Sails (@tailsnsails, etsy.com/shop/TailsnSails)

Instagram Photography with Jen Ha (p. 128-131)

Styling and photography by Jen Ha (@hellohoku)

How to Introduce Your Dog to a Carrier (p. 142)

Additional research, styling and photography by Sarah Dickerson (@chicsprinkles)

Additional pet products and props supplied by: Sleepypod (sleepypod.com)

Travel Hacks with Nikki Star (p. 160-163)

Styling and photography by Nikki Star (wheresthefrenchie.com)

How to Throw a Puppy Party (p. 166-169)

Styling and photography by Serena Faber-Nelson (prettyfluffy.com)

Models: Buddi (@buddi.the.mini.dachshund), Noodle (@noodle_the_cavoodle)

Additional pet products and props supplied by: Two Tails Pet Company (twotailspetcompany.com)

Zippy Paws (zippypaws.com)

Smash It! How to Do a Doggie Cake Smash (p. 170-172)

Additional research and photography by Lauren Dobish Photography (@laurcndobish, laurendobishphotography.com)

Models: Stella & Luna (@black.dog.sisters)

Scarves and bows: Tails & Sails (@tailsnsails, etsy.com/shop/TailsnSails)

How to Include Your Dog in a Wedding (p.174-177)

Photography by Lauren Dobish Photography (@laurendobish, laurendobishphotography.com)
Pet Coordinator: For The Love of Paws (@fortheloveofpawsss, fortheloveofpawsboston.com)
Planning & Design: Jessica Hennessey Weddings (@jessicahennesseyweddings, www.jessicahennesseyweddings.com)
Puppies: Great Dog Rescue New England (@gdrne, www.gdrne.com)
Floral Design: Beach Plum Event & Floral Design (@beachplumfloral, jillian-landry-86pc.squarespace.com)
Wedding Gown (@willowbywatters, watters.com/willowby for @bhldn, www.bhldn.com)
Bridesmaids Gowns (@flairboston, flairbridesmaid.com, @jennyyoonyc, jennyyoo.com & @theiacouture, theiacouture.com)
Makeup: Veronica Nunes Freelance Makeup Artist (@veronicanunes_mua, makeupbyv.com & @hwmakeupartistry)
Hair: The Bridal Bar (@stephanie.bridal.bar of @the.bridal.bar, celhair.com)
Models (@amanda_ohkay, @mrkmca)

How to Prepare Your Dog for a Baby (A Dog Lovers' Guide) (p. 182-188)

Photography by Lauren Dobish Photography (@laurendobish, laurendobishphotography.com)

Pet Memorials

Orchid Valley Pet Memorial. (p. 191)
Photography by Orchid Valley Pet Co. (ovpc.com.au)

silhouPETte Custom Charm. (p. 191) Styling and photography by Sarah Dickerson (@chicsprinkles)

Entertaining with Pets with Abby Capalbo (p. 194-197)

Styling by Abby Capalbo (abbycapalbo.com)
Photography by Erin McGinn Photography (erinmcginn.com)

Choosing Quality Pet Products with Jen Glaser (p. 204-207)

Photography by Morgan Kelly (bymorgankelly.squarespace.com)

About the Author (p. 217)

Photography by Petal Photography (petalphotography.com.au)

'Dog Mamas' Interior Cover Pages (Front—From Top L-R)

@fromgreatbeginnings
@hugo_the_newfie
@nycdogmom
@pretty_fluffy
@sweetbakeshop
@tmistick
@whatenzodid
@yellowbrickhome
@zarakellie
@_joycechristine
@thisdarlinghome
@whatenzodid
@chicsprinkles
@americasdogmom
@barkleydoodles
@allthefosterpups
@apieceoftoast
@bordernerd
@dognamedansel
@delucedesign

@bordernerd
@charlieandfrankie_
@delucedesign
@indiana_miniaussie
@kendallalex
@dood_itscharlie
@emjohnsonn
@buddi.the.mini.dachshund
@holdenthegolden_
@jsaraceno
@ladiesman.leo
@littlejerryboy
@fatmumslim
@madpuplife
@melislauren
@ksutherlandpr
@ladiesman.leo
@littlejerryboy
@maddison_ceccato
@madpuplife
@mr.p_thedappleddachshund
@nycdogmom
@pizzazzerie
@pretty_fluffy
@prouddogmomblog
@motherduckinggoose
@organicpetco
@shaynnablaze
@prettysweetlife
@drakelovespippa
@puppynamedcharlie
@saffronavenue
@sweetbakeshop
@the.goldie.locks
@thedogmomchronicles
@saffronavenue
@thebarkblogger
@tailsnsails
@forthefurry
@willow_thegreat

'Dog Mamas' Interior Cover Pages (Back—From Top L-R)

@zarakellie
@amayadamico
@americasdogmom
@bordernerd
@bordernerd
@zarakellie
@zarakellie
@americasdogmom
@barriespaws
@bordernerd
@capreek
@christine.loya
@dingo79
@drkatrina
@girlandthewolfphotography
@capreek
@casey_m_allen
@chicideology
@delucedesign
@drakelovespippa
@hannahkateroberts
@imlittlespoons
@jessicasuevelyn
@kendallalex
@kylieslarson
@forthefurry
@gooseberrystudios
@idpetaustralia
@jenkoala
@jsaraceno
@laur_k_weller
@leo_thebordercollie
@littlejerryboy
@madpuplife
@maggiejamesyoga
@ksutherlandpr
@ladiesman.leo
@layke_the_frenchie
@littlejerryboy

@charlenep81
@melislauren
@mr.p_thedappleddachshund
@noodle_the_cavoodle
@pawdinkum
@puppies.n.pinot
@madpuplife
@marienauseliebe
@mr_fetching
@oiliruffo
@pippa.blossom

@reggietheshepherd
@tara_jade29
@the.goldie.locks
@thisdarlinghome
@whereswallyh
@puppies.n.pinot
@seejaxgo
@thecuriouscollie
@thisdarlinghome
@ziggiandmuffin

Thank You

Writing a book isn't for the fainthearted. Writing a book while going through pregnancy is slightly mad. When my lovely publisher approved the pitch for *Dog Mama*, I found out I was pregnant just a week later. So for the next nine months I'd been nurturing two "projects." this book, and my gorgeous daughter.

Of course things never go to plan, and my pregnancy was complicated by severe hyperemesis and my daughter was born seven weeks early. For those reasons I need, first and foremost, to thank the kind and dedicated staff of The Mater Hospital in Sydney, Australia—especially the lovely midwives and doctors of the Special Care Nursery. Your exceptional care for my family and me during this time allowed me to recover and to be able to finish this book.

They say it "takes a village" and *Dog Mama* simply would not exist if it wasn't for the time and generosity of the talented individuals who contributed to this book.

To the entire team at Skyhorse Publishing, thank you for giving me the opportunity to write a second book. To my editors, Leah Zarra and Abigail Gehring, thank you for your continued guidance and believing in this project.

To the readers and followers of *Pretty Fluffy*. This book exists solely because of your continued support. And to all the dog mamas who shared their favorite photos to make our end papers so amazing—thank you!

Alex of Alexander Mayes Photography (@alexandermayesphotography), thank you again for bringing unbridled enthusiasm to our shoots and always capturing the exact shots I'm after. You're a joy to work with, and I'm proud to call you a friend.

To Bonnie Hindmarsh and the team at Three Birds Renovations (@threebirdsrenovations), thank you for welcoming us into your stunning home to shoot the cover and accompanying images.

To our dog mama models, Georgia & Jerry (@littlejerryboy) and Lauren & Indiana (@indiana _miniaussie), thank you for being so gracious with your time—I couldn't have asked for more beautiful dog mama shots than we got with you.

To Lauren Dobish (@laurendobish), thank you for your gorgeous photography used throughout this book. You're a true talent and an absolute joy to work with.

To all the pups featured in this book, thank you to you and your families for allowing us to capture your cuteness and share it with the world.

Thank you to the insanely talented Riley Sheehey (@cestriley) for allowing me to use your beautiful illustrations—as soon as I saw them I knew they'd be perfect! And thank you to Leigh Eisenman at MacKenzie Wolf for your assistance through the licensing process—it was a pleasure.

To our featured dog mamas, Stephanie (@stephsterjovski), Sarah (@chicsprinkles), Maitri (@honeyidressedthepug), Jen H. (@hellohoku), Nikki (@wtfrenchie), Abby (@abbycapalbo) and Jen G. (@jenkoala)—thank you for being part of the book and sharing your extensive expertise with our dog-loving audience.

To the generous brands that supplied product for our photo shoots—the teams at Zippy Paws (@zippypaws), Mister Woof (@mister.woof), Two Tails Pet Company (@twotailspetcompany), For the Furry (@forthefurry), The Foggy Dog (@thefoggydog), and Dyson (@dyson)—I can't thank you enough!

To Dr. Katrina Warren (@drkatrina) and editor of *Modern Dog Magazine*, Jennifer Nosek (@moderndogmag), thank you both for your assistance and valued feedback.

Last but certainly not least, thank you to my family and friends.

To our thoughtful friends and family who brought us food, sent messages of support and love over the last few months—we're lucky to have you.

To my longtime friends Brett Bowman (@imbrettbowman) and Alana Augustine, thank you for your wonderful advice that made the final drafts of *Dog Mama* better than before.

To my in-laws, Denis and Susan, who kindly offered babysitting (and dog sitting!) during shoot days. Thank you.

To Butterscotch, our beautiful boy. Thanks for posing like a superstar and being the beautiful furry sweetheart you are.

To Sarah Dickerson (@chicsprinkles), what would I be without your support, input, and guidance? You, my friend, are the ultimate dog mama. Your contributions throughout this book—DIY projects you created, photos you styled, and your masterful input into the design and layout of this entire project—have all been above and beyond. I truly admire your talent, kindness, and faith. I'm beyond lucky to work with you, but even luckier to call you a friend. Thank you for everything and I look forward to a lifetime of friendship.

To my husband, Andy, thank you for proofreading each and every word, visiting the flower markets for props at 5:00 a.m., and believing in me every step of the way. Love you.

And to my baby girls, Emmy and Isobel. I'm certainly a proud dog mama, but I'm also proud to be your mama. I love you and look forward to seeing all you will do in the world. Thank you for inspiring me to be the best I can be.

About the Author

SERENA FABER-NELSON is the founder of the internationally popular pet lifestyle destination, *Pretty Fluffy*, an online home where dedicated dog owners find stylish products, modern advice, and inspiration for living well with their pets. She has contributed to publications such as *Every Day with Rachael Ray*, *Modern Dog Magazine*, *Cesar's Way*, and more. Serena currently lives in Sydney, Australia, with her young family and dog.

www.prettyfluffy.com

 @pretty_fluffy

f @prettyfluffy

Also by Serena Faber-Nelson:

Healthy Homemade Dog Treats: More than 70 Delicious, Simple & Nourishing Recipes for Your Furry Best Friend